Warman's

POLITICAL

★ COLLECTIBLES ★

Dr. Enoch

All photos by Doug Mitchel

e Guide

©2008 Dr. Enoch L. Nappen

Published by

kp krause publications
An Imprint of F+W Publications

700 East State Street • Iola, WI 54990-0001
715-445-2214 • 888-457-2873
www.krausebooks.com

Our toll-free number to place an order or obtain a free catalog is (800) 258-0929.

Library of Congress Control Number: 2007942603
ISBN-13: 978-0-89689-624-6
ISBN-10: 0-89689-624-2

Designed by Sandy Kent
Edited by Joe Kertzman

Printed in China

🎗 DEDICATION 🎗

I dedicate this book to my wife, Barbara, and my children, Evan, Louis and Hillary, who patiently encouraged and tolerated my adventurous outings in search of political history.

🎗 ACKNOWLEDGMENTS 🎗

My effort could never have started without those students of political history who did some of the original research on their subject, including J. Doyle DeWitt, Russell Rulau, Neil MacNeil, J. R. Burdick and Herbert R. Collins. I must also thank those who stimulated awareness of political collectibles, through their books and auctions, and of the vast variety of material out there waiting to be discovered and conserved, in particular Ted Hake and the late Leon Wiesel.

Author Enoch L. Nappen

TABLE OF CONTENTS

INTRODUCTION

In some respects, current political campaigning is dull and limited compared to the creative promotional techniques of the past. Nowadays presidential campaigns tend to concentrate money and resources in television advertising. Mail-outs and postcards are used, but since 1968, political buttons are mostly made for collectors.

Relatively few people actually wear political buttons at all, let alone don them throughout an entire election campaign. Some of the old techniques are still used, yet the most popular contemporary political items are the ubiquitous bumper stickers and yard signs that crop up every election cycle.

My goal is to illustrate the tremendous, full variety of campaign and historic political memorabilia that has been used throughout American politics. This book is not designed to present a complete descriptive record of all our past elections, but instead to discuss and display the major categories of campaign material.

Political campaign items embody the entire economic and social life of their eras. They include items used in day-to-day living, from thimbles and watch fobs to toys and apparel. Such political items reveal long-gone social, economic and manufacturing conditions, as well as the political issues and celebrities of their day.

I was one of the early members of the American Political Items Collectors association (APIC). As a young political science professor teaching at Monmouth University, I became increasingly interested in political campaign material. I would search flea markets for items to illustrate one of my courses, Political Parties and Elections.

In the process of searching for election and issue campaign items (before they were so popular to collect), I came to realize that a complete understanding of politics and American history required looking beyond formal campaign literature.

I was amazed to discover that almost every area of collector interest included campaign material. Postcards, jewelry, photography, textiles, medals, toys and ceramics were just a part of the enormous variety of items available. It became clear that a total communication effort meant that political campaigners ignored no phase of social and economic daily life.

Ephemeral items are often more revealing of our changing society and its evolving values than any formal statue or marble memorial could ever be. In the absence of radio and particularly television, the early campaign efforts had to be clever. They creatively had to grab and hold the attention of their audience.

Political advertising involves more than major national party activities. Items supporting presidential hopefuls—those who tried to win Republican or Democratic Party nominations—are also of great collector interest. A state campaign item would be particularly prized if that local candidate later ran for president or was pictured with a presidential candidate on a coattail button. Most old minor party campaign material is frequently as, if not more, difficult and costly to obtain.

Over the years, a number of books have dealt mostly with campaign buttons. The buttons are often beautifully designed and have grown significantly in value. A number of the truly rare items may auction for thousands of dollars. I have always believed that the more rare they are, the less likely they were aggressively used in an election.

It is more fun collecting ignored bargains. Buttons are great, but why limit your interest? There are still hundreds of historic and contemporary items available at flea markets, antique stores, shows and auctions that are often not considered important and, as a result, are either trashed or sold for a fraction of their future historic worth. Save them and you save what the history books, unfortunately, usually ignore.

For the collector of political memorabilia, these items have excellent investment potential. It is my hope that this book increases public awareness and gives you—the reader—a collector's advantage.

VALUES

Value appears to depend on design, rarity, condition, and the candidates or issues involved. Cost may simply depend on two people aggressively bidding for the same item. When I started collecting political and campaign memorabilia, there were three major considerations: (1) preserving artifacts of American history that nonchalantly were being destroyed; (2) the pleasure in recognizing the persons or events that the items represented; and (3) using the pieces as illustrations in my political parties class or as home wall decorations.

There was no pleasure in having a dealer tell me what something was (unless the information was new to me) and what it was worth. Eventually, I realized that the collection was also an investment. It was then an added pleasure in buying a bargain or, at least, at a reasonable cost.

Cost and value are not necessarily the same. Ultimately, the value depends on one's own perception. An item may have much more value than its existing likely cost. For purposes of this book, I have included "likely costs," but the values ultimately depend on the reader.

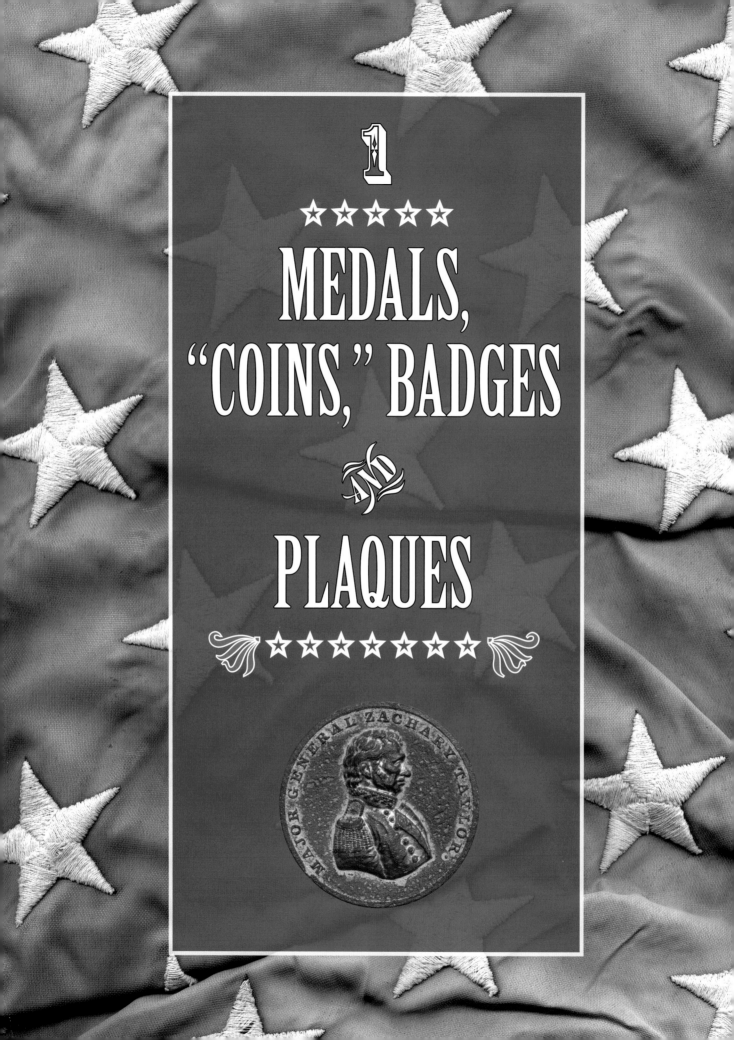

1

⬠ ★ ★ ★ ★ ⬠

MEDALS, "COINS," BADGES

AND

PLAQUES

★ ★ ★ ★ ★ ★ ★ ★ ★ ★

A running jackass and the phrase "I Follow In The Steps Of My Illustrious Predecessor" refers to Martin Van Buren continuing Andrew Jackson's policies, **$35-$60**.

mall metallic tokens constituted one of the earliest mass-production campaign categories intended to capture the growing electorate's attention and vote. As revealed in this chapter, the qualities and directions of these items changed over the years according to the country's industrial and commercial development, social conditions and political realignments. The coins, medals, badges and plaques weren't even necessarily traditional metals. As celluloid, aluminum and other composites became available, they were quickly adopted.

Some pieces were used as money. Others were worn on outer garments, carried as pocket tokens, or simply displayed with pride on shelves and walls. They might be given away or sold to anyone, or only worn by the party's official convention delegates. They might even be carried privately and secretly to show or identify fellow supporters.

The Hard Times Token depicts Andrew Jackson emerging from a chest and holding a sword and moneybag. The allusion is to Jackson's effort to control money and the military, **$35-$60**.

Ultimately, they could be used to criticize and ridicule opponents, or praise candidates and simply display party loyalty. Whatever their purpose or design, they represent American democracy in action.

Under the premise that the Ship of State is a symbol of the country, currency and money flow, the Martin Van Buren ship is portrayed as either striking rocks or hit by lightning. The reverse side of the Hard Times Token shows the Daniel Webster ship sailing smoothly, **$35-$60**.

The tortoise and safe refer to the problems resulting from Martin Van Buren's movement of money, **$35-$60**.

"Am I Not A Woman & A Sister" is an early anti-slavery piece from 1838, **$35-$60**.

"Specie Payments Suspended" refers to Andrew Jackson's 1836 requirement that only gold and silver would be accepted for western land sales, **$35-$60**.

"To meet demand, millions of Civil War tokens were privately issued as money substitutes."

HARD TIMES TOKENS

During the first quarter of the 19th century, there were a number of limited-production pieces honoring George Washington and other early American presidents.

However, the first mass production of election material began with the emergence of Andrew Jackson's Democratic Party and the counter emergence of the Whigs. The party divide was particularly apparent with the issuing of copper one-cent money substitutes during the economic difficulties and hoarding of the 1832-1844 period.

Many of the "coins," referred to as "Hard Times Tokens," were embossed with the businesses that offered the substitute money as change. Other such tokens looked like the large liberty head cent of the time (about 28 mm), but with the opposite side of the token reading "Not One Cent."

A large number and variety were clever satirical tokens aggressively attacking Andrew Jackson and his successor Martin Van Buren. With clever symbolism, they ridiculed the Democratic Party, and Jackson in particular, for the disastrous economy.

So many of the political Hard Times Tokens were produced that most are relatively inexpensive in average condition. The ones illustrated would now probably sell for $35 to $60 each. In superb condition or of a rare variety, each would sell for considerably more. The best book on merchant tokens is Russell Rulau's *Standard Catalog of United States Tokens 1700-1900*, Krause Publications Inc., Iola, WI, 1994. See pp. 69-88 for a thorough study and coverage of all Hard Times Tokens.

"Substitute for Shin Plasters" copper tokens were superior to privately issued, worthless paper fractional currency. Claiming that shinplasters were only good for burning, the Phoenix design implied better conditions would emerge from their destruction, **$35-$60**.

The stubborn jackass refers to the perception that Andrew Jackson used presidential vetoes, not because he thought the proposed law was unconstitutional, but merely because he did not like it. The "LLD" was placed on a jackass to ridicule Jackson's honorary Harvard degree (LLD), **$35-$60**.

This pro-Andrew Jackson piece on the left is arguably one of the earliest campaign medals, 1824, 24 mm. The piece on the right is one of the relatively few pro-Jackson Hard Times Tokens, circa 1832, 26 mm, **$50-$100** each. Nineteenth-century medal and ferrotype badges are traditionally measured in millimeters, whereas celluloid buttons and ribbons are measured in inches.

The pro-Martin Van Buren tokens, circa 1836-'40, would go for approximately **$30-$50** each today, with the larger piece on the higher end.

The William Henry Harrison election was the earliest aggressive example of a modern campaign, thus many of his tokens were produced and are still relatively common, circa 1840, **$20-$50** each, depending on condition and size.

Perhaps because James Polk was the first "Dark Horse" (unpredicted convention winner) and did not run for a second term, his campaign medals are rare and difficult to obtain, white medal, 1844, 39 mm, **$100-$200**.

SAMPLING OF EARLY MEDALS (1844-1864)

Before the 1860 presidential election, miniature campaign items consisted mostly of brass clothing buttons or medals, usually with holes through them at the top to facilitate wearing. A string or thin ribbon would be passed through the hole and then fastened directly to outer clothing.

Finding these pieces with holes does not mean they have been damaged. The best, most thorough early study of small political items was *A Century of Campaign Buttons 1789-1889*, written and privately published by J. Doyle DeWitt.

Whig Presidential candidate Winfield Scott brass badge, circa 1852, rare.

Democratic Presidential candidate Lewis Cass brass medal, circa 1848, rare.

⭐ **Most of the following medals would sell for $30-$65 each, depending on condition.**

"Henry Clay of Kentucky," white medal, circa 1830s, 36 mm.

"I Would Rather Be Right Than Be President/ H. Clay," brass medal, 1848, 24 mm.

"Henry Clay And The American System," copper medal, 1840, 28 mm.

"Henry Clay The Ashland Farmer," brass medal, 1844, 24 mm.

Maj. Gen. Zachary Taylor white medal, 1848, 41 mm.

"Major General Zachary Taylor" copper medal listing military victories, 1848, 25 mm.

"Gen. Frank Pierce The Statesman & Soldier" profile brass medal, 1852, 26 mm.

"Gen. Franklin Pierce The Statesman & Soldier" brass medal, 1852, 28 mm.

"Gen. Winfield Scott/ First In War First In Peace," brass medal, 1852, 30 mm.

"Maj. General Winfield Scott," brass medal, 1852, 26 mm.

"James Buchanan No Sectionalism," brass medal, 1856, 28 mm.

"Millard Fillmore For The Whole Country," brass medal, 1956, 29 mm.

"John C. Fremont. Free Soil & Free Speech," brass medal, 1856, 28 mm.

"J.C. Fremont Born Jan 21, 1813," brass medal, 1856, 23 mm.

"John Bell, Union Candidate For The Presidency," brass medal, 1860, 28 mm.

Hon. Stephen A. Douglas brass medal, 1860, 32 mm.

"Democratic Candidate Stephen A. Douglas 1860," brass medal, 28 mm.

This anti-Jefferson Davis brass medal portrays him being executed via a gallows hanging, with the reverse of the medal (not shown) reading "Death to Traitors," 1861, 25 mm.

Six Abraham Lincoln medals: five beardless Lincoln brass medals (31 mm; 28 mm w/reverse rural scene showing him splitting rails; 28 mm depicting on obverse and reverse uniformed Harford Wide Awakes Club member with his lantern or torch; 28 mm; and 28 mm), ca 1860, and one bearded Lincoln white medal with reverse reading "Freedom To All Men/Union," 1864, 32 mm, **$60-85** each, with the exception of the popular rail splitter going for **$100-$150**.

Four different George McClellan medals: three of white metal (34 mm, with flag ribbon; 32 mm with reverse stressing "The Constitution As It Is;" and 28 mm) and one copper medal with a blank space within a wreath. The latter medal was possibly used as a dog tag, increasing its value, 32 mm, circa 1864.

BRASS SHANK BUTTONS AND STUDS

Brass shank buttons with embossed names or features of candidates were actually used as clothing buttons. Most would sell for **$35-$60** apiece, with Henry Clay pieces being on the high end.

Three brass shank buttons created for William Henry Harrison's campaign, each featuring a log cabin and barrel, 1840, 20-21 mm.

Brass button displaying a liberty cap, "E Pluribus Unum," and "Whigs of 76 & 34," 13 mm.

Two similar brass images of Henry Clay, one made as a hanging piece with the reverse side reading "Clay & Frelinghuysen Protection & Union," 1844, 24 mm. The other is enclosed as a shank button, 24 mm.

Two "Rough & Ready," Zachary Taylor brass shank buttons, 1848, 23 mm. One reads "The Hero Of Buena Vista" on the reverse side.

Garfield and Arthur brass shank button, 1880, 21 mm.

Hancock and English brass shank button, 1880, 21 mm.

Rooster brass shank button, Democratic Club symbol, circa 1880, 21 mm.

Blaine & Logan brass shank button with plumed knight, Blaine's campaign symbol, 1884, 19 mm.

Cleveland & Hendricks brass shank button, 1884, 19 mm.

"H & M," brass shank button, with the letters likely standing for Harrison and Morton, 14 mm.

"C & S," shank button with overlapping initials for Cleveland and Stevenson, circa 1892, 22 mm.

William McKinley and Theodore Roosevelt brass shank button, 1900, 14 mm.

By the late 1880s, there was a clear movement away from shank buttons and toward studs. These are examples of Benjamin Harrison metal studs for the 1888 election, **$25-$35** each.

COUNTER STAMPED COIN

As an advertising ploy during the 19th century, merchants counter stamped their business or product name on circulating coinage. These were considered junk coins 50 years ago, and now they are very popular.

CIVIL WAR TOKENS

During the Civil War, hoarding magnified military and economic doubts. To meet demand, millions of Civil War tokens were privately issued as money substitutes. They were usually the same size and design as Indian cents, but they frequently advertised specific businesses as well as political and patriotic support.

Common, average-condition tokens sell for about **$10**. They could, however, sell for 10 or more times that amount, depending on the business, the state, the metal and condition. Abraham Lincoln and George McClellan Civil War tokens usually reach **$25-$40**, with Lincoln items often being more desirable.

"Vote The Land Free," counter stamped on a United States cent, circa 1848, 27½ mm, **$50-$75**.

Four examples of Abraham Lincoln Civil War tokens, circa 1963-'64.

Shown are seven examples of George McClellan Civil War tokens and one Stephen Douglas token. Sometimes the obverse of the coins was the same, but with different reverse sides (second tokens from left, top and bottom rows, with example of a reverse side shown). Far left top row reverse reads "McClellan medal for one cent".

CAMPAIGN MEDALS (1868-1892)

A large variety of copper, brass and white metal medals were issued each presidential election cycle. Following is a representative sampling in the **$35-$75** range.

Four different Ulysses S. Grant medals: three white medals (32 mm, 28 mm hanging from an eagle pin, and 28 mm), and one brass medal, 28 mm, circa 1868 -'72.

Horace Greeley brass medal, 1872, 24 mm.

Horatio Seymour brass *jugate* (showing the presidential and vice-presidential candidates) medal with Francis P. Blair, 1868, 28 mm.

Rutherford B. Hayes copper medal, 1876, 31 mm, **$100-$150**.

Two Samuel Tilden medals include a copper campaign medal, 1876, 31 mm, and a satirical white medal, circa 1877, 31 mm.

Four James Garfield medals, with two white medals (inauguration medal, 1881, 33 mm and a portrait medal with reverse depiction of name GAR over FIELD, an appeal to Union veterans with "GAR" standing for Grand Army of the Republic, 1880, 25 mm); and two brass medals, one a profile with Chester A. Arthur, and a portrait medal with reverse depicting his rise from canal boy to the White House, 25 mm.

Three Maj. Gen. Winfield Hancock medals (two brass and one white metal) show him in military uniform, and two feature the three-leaf-clover symbol of his military unit, circa 1880, 25 mm.

Five James Blaine medals include three profile medals with John Logan (white metal, 31 mm and two brass pieces, 26 mm); one white medal hanging from an eagle pin, 28mm; and one white medal depicting the "white plume" knight (his campaign symbol), 26 mm, circa 1884.

Featured are three Grover Cleveland jugate (showing the presidential and vice-presidential candidates) profile medals: two with Thomas Hendricks (one white metal, 31 mm and one brass, 26 mm), 1884; and one with Adlai Stevenson, aluminum medal, 1892, 30 mm.

Three Grover Cleveland portrait medals feature reverse sides stressing reform—honesty in government and lowering tariffs. Two are white metal (29 mm hanging from eagle pin and 28 mm), and one is brass, 26 mm, circa 1884.

Two post-Democratic National Convention pieces: a white medal depicting Jefferson, Jackson, Tilden, Cleveland and a rooster (the Party symbol), 1888, 45 mm; and an aluminum medal depicting the Democratic nominees Cleveland and Adlai Stevenson above the White House, 1892, 45 mm.

Cleveland and his popular young bride were depicted in three brass medals. Two particularly deal with their tour through the West and South during October 1887, 26 mm.

Five Benjamin Harrison medals, one white metal, 1888, 38 mm; and four portrait medals (one brass medal, 1888, 21 mm; one white medal with reverse reading "Protection and Reciprocity," circa 1888-'92; one brass jugate medal hanging from eagle pin with reverse reading "Protection to Home Industries," 1888, 25 mm; and one brass medal hanging from ribbon with reverse reading "Protection To American Labor," 1892, 25 mm. The medals stress, in different ways, the major Republican issue of the time—protective tariffs.

EARLY NON-METALLIC MEDALS

Grover Cleveland and Thomas Hendricks hard rubber badge, circa 1884, 36 mm, **$75-$125**.

James Blaine and John Logan hard-rubber, dark-brown and light-brown badges, circa 1884, 36 mm, **$75-$125**.

"I'm For Harrison. R-U?" hard rubber with an image of Benjamin Harrison and reverse advertising the Plymouth Rock Pants Co., circa 1892, 38 mm, **$75-$100**.

"Stephen A. Douglas," composition material similar to daguerreotype cases with his image, circa 1860, 26 mm, **$200-$300**.

"I'm For Cleveland. R-U?" hard rubber with an image of Grover Cleveland and reverse advertising the Plymouth Rock Pants Co., circa 1892, 38 mm, **$75-$100**.

CELLULOID

With the increased commercial development of celluloid during the mid-1880s, it was soon applied to the manufacturing of campaign items and produced to simulate an opaque, expensive "ivory" look with the candidate's picture printed on top.

A Grover Cleveland and two Benjamin Harrison images on celluloid and attached to studs, circa 1888, 17 mm, **$25-$35** each.

Benjamin Harrison and Levi Morton pictured with their wives on celluloid sheet, circa 1888-'92, 3" x 6⅞", **$25-$35**.

ALUMINUM

During most of the 19th century, aluminum was rare and costly, but by the late 1880s significantly reduced production cost led to its quick adoption as a campaign tool. In contrast to "white metal" which looked beautiful new, but dented and turned an ugly dark color, aluminum political medals were so amazingly light, yet strong, that they attracted and held the attention of voters.

These two Benjamin Harrison campaign medals look exactly alike, but the medal on the right is aluminum, "Smith & Seward Makers," circa 1892, 30 mm, **$35-$50** each.

The pie-cut aluminum medal addresses the major Republican issue of the day— the protective tariff. It reads "Your Wages Under Free Trade," with the reverse saying "What Matter If Prices Are Reduced If Wages Drop To Free Trade Levels?" Circa 1888-'92, 38 mm, **$30-$40**.

An aluminum caricature medal sarcastically features a lady riding a donkey and other illustrated commentary to criticize Bryan's plan, 1900, 37 mm, **$35-$50**.

BRYAN 16-TO-1 DOLLAR MEDALS

William Jennings Bryan's "Cross of Gold" speech at the 1896 Democratic convention went so well that he won the nomination. Bryan wanted silver as well as gold to be the monetary standard, envisioning silver coined in a 16-to-1 ratio with gold, supposedly spreading prosperity and reducing Depression debt.

Republican critics stressed that this would hurt investors, businesses and the economy in general. Republican William McKinley's key personal issue was maintaining a protective tariff, but he strongly endorsed gold as the only monetary standard.

The "absurdity" of Bryan's plan was satirized by making crude medals that exaggerated the size of the silver dollar if coined at a 16-to-1 ratio with gold.

Most of the "Bryan Dollars" looked similar to the Morgan silver dollars, but were made of base metal and showcased the letters NIT ("Not In Trust") in the design, circa 1896, size varies slightly between 83 and 87 mm, **$100-$125** each.

Rare.

Silver Bryan Dollar, which on one side portrays the size of a real silver 16-to-01 "dollar," The Gorham Manufacturing Co., circa 1896, 51 mm, **$100-$150**.

William McKinley mechanical dollars were made in both 1896 and 1900. The loops at the tops of such coins were action levers. With the eagle on each coin in the upright position, the message on the reverse side of the coin reads "Gold Standard Means A Dollar Worth 100 Cents" or "Sound Money Means A Dollar Worth 100 Cents." If the lever is moved, the eagle bends down and the message reads "Free Silver Means A Dollar Worth 50 Cents," 37 mm, **$50-$75** each.

UNOFFICIAL INAUGURATION BADGES

The following unofficial inauguration badges are valued at **$25-$60** each.

George McClellan inauguration badge portrays him when he was Governor of New Jersey, January 15, 1878.

Benjamin Harrison badge, 1889.

"Courage/ Consistency," brass badge featuring profiles of Cleveland and his wife, circa 1893.

"American Tariff Reform Champion," brass badge with Grover Cleveland profile, circa 1893.

Franklin D. Roosevelt brass badge picturing Roosevelt as the 32nd President, 1933.

Harry Truman brass badge, Jan. 20, 1949 (20th Amendment moved the inauguration date from March 4 to Jan. 20.)

Grover Cleveland brass badge missing pin bar and ribbon, 1893.

William McKinley brass badge, 1897.

William H. Taft badge with a ½" brass metal in the middle, 1909.

Woodrow Wilson brass badge missing pin bar and ribbon, 1917.

William H. Taft heart-shaped brass badge, 1909.

Calvin Coolidge badge missing pin bar and ribbon, 1925.

Grover Cleveland brass badge, 1893.

William H. Taft brass badge, 1909.

Calvin Coolidge brass badge, 1925.

William McKinley brass badge, 1897.

NINETEENTH-CENTURY BADGES AND PLAQUE

The following badges are valued at approximately **$35-$70** each.

"1884," overlapping "C & H," enamel-inlaid brass badge for Cleveland and Hendricks, circa 1884.

"B/ L/ 84," enamel-inlaid brass badge for Blaine and Logan, circa 1884.

Embossed, silvered brass Benjamin Harrison badge hanging from a plated eagle, 1888.

William McKinley brass badge reading "Railroad Men's McKinley Club/Ft. Wayne, Ind." and hanging from a railroad engine-shaped pin, 1896-1900, **$80-$100**.

William McKinley brass badge reading "National Peace Jubilee/ Philadelphia" and hanging from a handshake pin, 1898.

Admiral George Dewey brass badge welcoming "The National Hero" and with reverse showing his Flag Ship *Olympia*, circa 1899-1900.

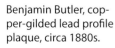

Benjamin Butler, copper-gilded lead profile plaque, circa 1880s.

"Blaine" brass script badge, circa 1884.

An early example of a lithographic, colored metal pin for Benjamin Harrison, circa 1888-'92, 24 x 35 mm, **$30-$50**.

"Cleveland" brass script badge, circa 1884.

POLITICAL CONVENTION BADGES

A major responsibility at national party conventions was checking delegate credentials to insure valid voting rights. This could be crucial as in the 1912 Republican Convention when different sets of delegates claimed they represented several of the same states, resulting in the Republican Party split and Woodrow Wilson's election.

Delegates, alternates and a host of other functionaries usually wore official badges identifying their status. The great variety of badge designs is revealed in the following examples, which are in the **$35-$60** apiece range, except where noted

Republican badges from 1901, 1908,1912 and1920, Democratic badges from years 1908 and 1916, and a suffrage badge from 1920, **$75-$125** each.

Republican badges from 1924 and 1932, and Democratic badges from years 1928 and 1932, **$40-$75** apiece.

Democrat Convention badge and two Republican badges, 1936.

Democrat Convention badge and two Republican badges, 1940.

Two Democrat Convention badges and a Republican badge, 1944.

GREEN DUCK COMPANY
CHICAGO
World's Foremost Manufacturers of Badges, Advertising Buttons, Metal Advertising Novelties, Emblems.

Two Republican badges, including a congressman's, 1948.

"The economy has always been a hot topic in politics and political campaigning, particularly when the economy is bad."

Democrat Convention badges from 1952 and 1956, and a 1956 Republican badge.

Democrat Convention badges 1956, 1960 and 1964, and a 1964 Republican badge.

PRESIDENTIAL INAUGURATION MEDALS

Presidential inauguration medals honor newly elected presidents. Neil MacNeil's well-researched and illustrated book *The Presidential Medal 1789-1977*, Clarkson N. Potter, Inc., New York, 1977, expanded the appreciation of their history, artistic beauty and relative rarity. Some older examples follow.

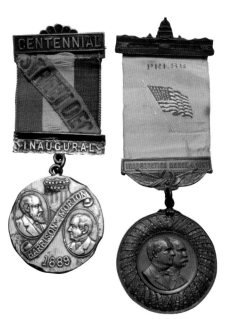

The Benjamin Harrison and Levi Morton badge is one of the earliest, officially commissioned presidential inauguration medals, white metal with images of both men, 1889, 38 mm, **$50-$75**.

Far right: An early, officially commissioned presidential inauguration medal, the William McKinley and Garret A. Hobart bronze badge features images of both men, 1897, 44 mm, **$100-$150**.

By 1901, the William McKinley Inauguration Committee decided to authorize the creation and purchase of medals for those taking an active part in the celebration, as revealed in the framed appointment to serve as an aid. Two copies of the inauguration medal are displayed on bottom left and right, 17½" x 21½" in original frame, **$400-$600**.

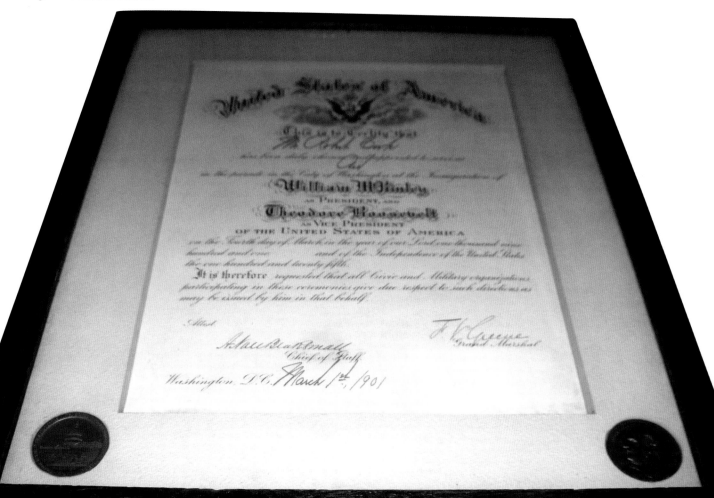

⭐ **All the following inauguration medals date back to 1901-1949 and are bronze unless noted otherwise.**

Harry Truman, 1949, 51 mm, **$150-$300**.

William McKinley, 1901, 44 mm, **$100-$150**.

Franklin Roosevelt medal, Jo Davidson, 1941, 45 mm, **$200-$300**.

Franklin Roosevelt profile bronze medal with reverse featuring *Old Ironsides* and reference to the "ship of state" (later used in clocks and lamps depicting Roosevelt as pilot leading the country to safety), "Paul Manship," 1933, 76mm, **$700-$900**.

Woodrow Wilson, 1913, 70 mm, **$150-$300**.

"William Jennings Bryan wanted silver as well as gold to be the monetary standard."

⭐ **The inauguration medals that follow date back to between 1953 and 1974.**

Dwight Eisenhower, 1953, 70 mm, **$30-$40**.

Dwight Eisenhower/ Richard Nixon, 1957, 70 mm, **$35-$50**.

John Kennedy silver medal, 1961, 70 mm, **$100-$150**.

Lyndon Johnson, 1965, 70 mm, **$25-$35**.

Richard Nixon silver medal, 1969, 64 mm, **$60-$80**.

Richard Nixon/ Spiro Agnew, 1973, 70 mm, **$25-$35**.

Gerald Ford vice-presidential silver medal, 1973, 63 mm, **$60-$90**.

Gerald Ford presidential silver medal, 1974, 63 mm, **$60-$90**.

Nelson Rockefeller silver vice president medal, 1974, 63 mm, **$60-$90**.

MINT MEDALS

Do not confuse the official inauguration medals with presidential medals made by the U.S. Mint. The Mint has offered re-strikes for sale. If the medal has a dark chocolate or dark copper finish, it may be a 19th-century piece. Original 20th-century medals have a darker bronze look. Re-strikes are either yellow bronze or sand blasted bronze in appearance.

Shown at right are two examples of older U. S. Mint medals.

Benjamin Harrison, U.S. Mint inauguration medal, 1889, 75 mm, **$50-$75**.

EMBOSSED METAL SHEETS

Calvin Coolidge, U.S. Mint inauguration medal, 1923, 74 mm, **$25-$40**.

"McKinley and Hobart," embossed brass medal reading "Sound Money And Protection," with pin on reverse for wearing, circa 1896, 2½" in diameter, **$50-$100**.

Admiral Dewey embossed brass medal hanging from brass eagle pin with cardboard backing reading "Wear this badge in honor of Admiral George Dewey the hero of Manila," "Samuel Ward Company," circa 1899-1900, 5½", **$50-$75** presidential hopeful.

William McKinley copper die-cut bust with pin on reverse for wearing, circa 1896-1900, 4¼" x 6", **$30-$50**.

Matching pair of Woodrow Wilson and Theodore Roosevelt embossed copper images in wooden frames for display, circa 1912, 4¾" x 6½", **$30-$50** each.

Alfred E. Smith, die-cut, embossed copper image of the Democratic U.S. presidential candidate wearing top hat embossed "W&H," 1928, 5¾" x 9", **$100-$150**.

KU KLUX KLAN MEDALS

The Ku Klux Klan originally developed as a secret society after the Civil War. During the 1920s, the Klan grew rapidly with the help of the book *The Klansman* and D.W. Griffith's pro-white-supremacist movie, "Birth of a Nation." The Klan grew so strong in and beyond the South that its support was often essential to win elections.

By 1924, the Klan was able to stop Alfred Smith from winning the Democratic presidential nomination. With later indictments and charges of corruption and scandal, Klan membership and influence dropped to a fraction of its previous position.

> "By 1924, the Ku Klux Klan was able to stop Alfred Smith from winning the Democratic presidential nomination."

Ku Klux Klan medals and center badge, circa 1920s, **$30-$50** each. According to Arlie R. Slabaugh's study of Klan medals, *The Journal of the Token and Medal Society, Vol. IV,* 1964, No. 1, pp. 11-17, the meanings of some of the letters or phrases are as follows:

Code	Supposed Meaning
1. *Non Silba Sed Anthar*	Not for self but for others
2. KIGY	Klansman, I greet you
3. The triangular IAKA	I am a Klansman

Alton Parker's image on an aluminum identification medal, 1904, 32 mm, rare.

KEY TAGS OR ADDRESS MEDALS

A key tag is a metal piece meant to be engraved or punched with the owner's name and address, and attached to keys. If lost, the keys would, in theory, be returned to their rightful owner or, as later feared, encourage burglars. Many stores issued business-advertising medals with different numbers struck for each customer. Lost keys would be mailed to the store that would then return them to the customer.

ELONGATED CENTS

An elongated cent is one that has been squeezed between two metal rollers, one of which is an engraved die, transforming it into a newly designed, thinner and elongated medal with the reverse side showing the "shadow" of the cent's original design. Dottie Dow directly increased their collector value through her privately published 1965 book *The Elongated Collector*.

Ku Klux Klan key tag, circa 1920s, 20 x 42 mm, **$30-$50**.

Wendell Willkie elongated cent, circa 1940, **$10-$20**.

John Kennedy elongated cent, circa 1960s, **$1-$2**.

Seven Franklin Roosevelt elongated cents, circa 1930s, **$10-$20** each.

Alton Parker elongated dime, circa 1904, **$25-$40**.

LARGE LUCKY SOUVENIR MEDALS

Starting before World War I and growing in popularity during the 1920s, souvenir venders sold large, exaggerated-size "coins" as trip mementoes.

"Two "Harding Lucky Penny," souvenirs with Warren G. Harding's image, 1921 and 1923, 70 mm, **$35-$60** each.

ECONOMIC COMPLAINT COINS

The economy has always been a hot topic in politics and political campaigning, particularly when the economy is bad, taking a downturn, or in a state of recession or depression. Coins issued in the 1920s, '30s, '40s and even '80s reflected just such an oppressed mood.

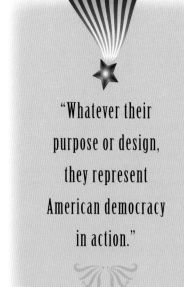

"Whatever their purpose or design, they represent American democracy in action."

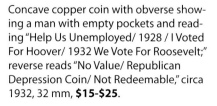Concave copper coin with obverse showing a man with empty pockets and reading "Help Us Unemployed/ 1928 / I Voted For Hoover/ 1932 We Vote For Roosevelt;" reverse reads "No Value/ Republican Depression Coin/ Not Redeemable," circa 1932, 32 mm, **$15-$25**.

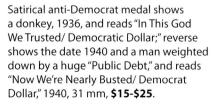Satirical anti-Democrat medal shows a donkey, 1936, and reads "In This God We Trusted/ Democratic Dollar;" reverse shows the date 1940 and a man weighted down by a huge "Public Debt," and reads "Now We're Nearly Busted/ Democrat Dollar," 1940, 31 mm, **$15-$25**.

Satirical anti-Democrat medal pictures a caricature of Lyndon Johnson and reads "The Great Society/ He Poorhouse Ruined Em/ 1984;" reverse pictures a donkey's rear and reads "Tyranny/ Nonsense/ Inflation We Trust," 1984, 38 mm **$5-$10**.

FLIPPING MEDALS

Flipping medals were novelty coins used to decide issues based on whether heads or tails faced up after flipping them.

Franklin Delano Roosevelt and John Nance Garner copper medal with profile images of the candidates and "Heads You Win/ Lucky Coin 1936," with reverse picturing an elephant's rear and "Tails You Lose," 31 mm, **$15-$25**.

Elephant head brass medal with words "Honesty/ Integrity," and the reverse side displaying a donkey rear with the words "Mink, 5%/ Deep Freeze, Tax Scandal," circa 1950s, 31 mm, **$10-$20**.

Elephant head medal with the words "Be Ahead In '48" and a donkey tail on the reverse side, 1948, 31 mm, **$10-$15**.

"The President Picker," medal with profile of Ronald Reagan and "Vote Reagan;" the flip side of the coin reveals a profile of Jimmy Carter with the words "Vote Carter;" and on both sides, in small letters, "If Coin Lands On Edge, Vote Anderson" (John B. Anderson, minor party candidate), 1980, 31 mm, **$5-$10**.

PERCEPTION OF VISION TOKENS

A "perception of vision token" is a medal that rotates freely inside a hanger. Each side of the piece has different letters or pictures, but when it spins rapidly, perception of vision results in both sides being seen at the same time, completing the wording or total picture.

Two spinners, if medal was spun, would display a donkey and elephant mating, 38 x 49 mm, **$5-$10** each.

Disk with individual letters that, when medal is spun, spell out "Roosevelt," but hanger is missing from this piece, 19 mm, **$5-$10**.

ENCASED COINS

Encased coins were usually aluminum advertisement or souvenir pieces enclosing a then-current cent and touting the slogan "Keep me and never go broke." Political encased coins are rather uncommon.

"I Like IKE," encased 1956 cent, 32 mm, **$5-$10** .

Encased nickel for the 1950 Jefferson Jubilee & Democratic National Conference incorporating the Harry Truman quote, "Our Goal Must Be Peace For All Time," 1950, 34 mm, **$15-$25**.

Kennedy-Johnson encased 1960 cents, 32 mm, **$10-$15**.

Encased cent for Lincoln Day Dinner, Feb. 16, 1952, Albany. NY, 34 mm, **$5-$10**.

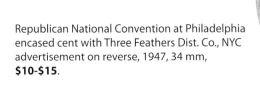

Republican National Convention at Philadelphia encased cent with Three Feathers Dist. Co., NYC advertisement on reverse, 1947, 34 mm, **$10-$15**.

"To meet demand, millions of Civil War tokens were privately issued as money substitutes."

WOODEN COINS

During the past 50 years, "wooden coins" have been relegated to being round disks encouraging business trade. Political pieces are much less common, but would only currently sell in the **$3-$5** range (after all, they are wooden nickels).

Lyndon Johnson wooden coin with reverse reading "Let Us Continue," circa 1964, 38 mm.

Pro-Richard Nixon wooden coin showcasing a smiling image of the candidate and reading "Nixon Dilemma;" reverse criticizes a hostile press and liberal politicians for crucifying him, circa1972-'74, 52 mm.

Barry Goldwater wooden coin featuring a flip side reading "A Choice For A Change," circa 1964, 38 mm.

STILL MORE TWENTIETH-CENTURY MEDALS & PLAQUES

National Republican Convention copper medal issued by the "Wm. R. Leeds Association," including Leeds' portrait on the obverse, 1904, 43 mm, **$20-$30**.

Woodrow Wilson portrait medal with reverse reading, in part, "American Red Cross Bazaar / Relief Fund For Soldiers, Women And Children," October 1914, 31 mm, **$20-$30**.

Franklin Delano Roosevelt copper medal similar to 1941 inauguration medal with reverse blank, Jo Davidson, 1941, 6¼" diameter, **$100-$200**.

Warren Harding bronze portrait medal struck for the 25th anniversary of the Keller Mechanical Engraving Co., 1921, 34 x 27 mm, **$40-$60**.

John Hylan (New York City Mayor) octagon portrait medal issued for the 1924 Democratic Convention, 58 x 58 mm, **$25-$40**.

"Roosevelt Reception June 18, 1910" copper fob with Theodore Roosevelt portrait, 31 mm, **$20-$35**.

Woodrow Wilson high-relief, large copper medal, circa 1910s, 13⅜", **$100-$150**.

Alfred Smith, Governor of New York copper plaque by Morgan Hinchman, 1928, 4 x 4¾", **$75-$100**.

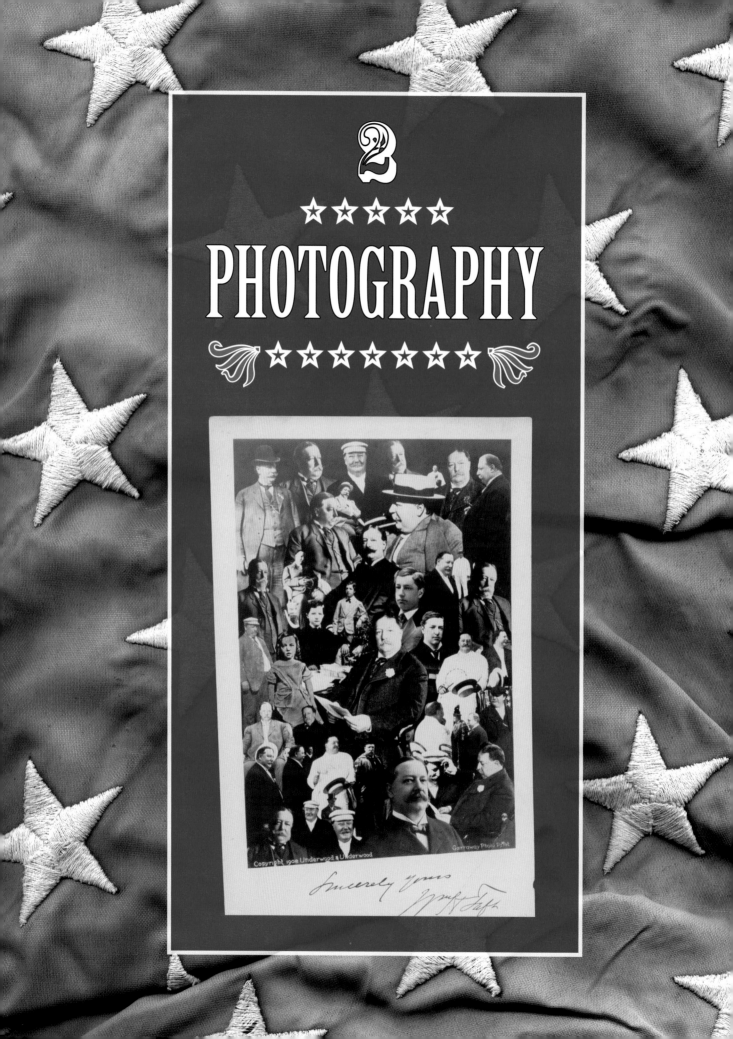

2

★ ★ ★ ★ ★

PHOTOGRAPHY

★ ★ ★ ★ ★ ★ ★ ★ ★ ★ ★

uring the second half of the 19th century, photography played an increasingly significant role in the presidential campaign process. Inventive pieces were produced in a multitude of creative forms. There was a commitment to creativity, style and wit in the photograph's mounting and display.

Photos were usually purchased at a nominal price or given away by political clubs. As ephemeral items, they were rarely meant to have any lasting significance or even survive more than the coming election. Those items that somehow did survive are colorful and revealing mementos of the period's social, economic and political life. Today, many are quite rare and valuable.

It is impossible to imagine the distribution of such pieces in many other 19th-century countries. The industrial revolution combined with American participatory democracy to flood the market with photographic "eye catchers". Fortunately as a result of their inherent charm, examples were saved. They have left a photographic history of the American political process, as well as a photographic record of the individual candidates.

A political button collector should be familiar with such major manufacturers as Whitehead and Hoag, Bastian Brothers, Philadelphia Badge Co. and Greenduck. Similarly, a photographic historian must recognize the names of numerous 19th-century photographers whose pictures are likely to be of the era's celebrities. Plumbe, Southworth & Hawes, Brady, Root, Gurney, Mora, Pach, Bogardus and Sarony were particularly noted for focusing on famous people.

Furthermore, the imprint of these photographers imparts a value to their pictures beyond the limits of their subjects. In other words, photographic collectors will gladly pay more for a Plumbe or a Brady even if the picture is somebody's Aunt Tillie.

This is a recently discovered sixth-plate daguerreotype of Dolly Madison, with a brass oval mat and half case, circa 1847, rare. Madison appears to be wearing the same clothing shown in the print of President Polk and Cabinet members illustrated in Harold Pfister's well-documented study *Facing the Light,* Smithsonian Institution Press, City of Washington, 1978, p. 70.

DAGUERREOTYPES

Daguerreotypes resulted from the most popular photographic technique during the 1840-1857 period. However, they had only limited direct value as campaign items since each daguerreotype was unique and rather expensive. Assuming the pose and processing were done properly, the portrait could be magnificent but the silver-plated image was still one of a kind.

Your likelihood of finding a political candidate's daguerreotype is extremely rare, but not impossible.

DAGUERREOTYPE PRINTS

Edward Anthony published what was probably one of the earliest uses of a photograph as a tool for presidential campaigning—a glass-framed engraving of Gen. Zachary Taylor made from a daguerreotype, "Thomas Doney," circa 1848, 5¾" x 4⅞", **$750-$1,000**.

Since daguerreotype portraits rarely provide positive identification of the subjects posing for the photographs, one must cross-reference other published photos to uncover the people's identities. Although daguerreotypes are usually older than published photos, and thus the subjects in the photos are younger than they appear in circulated publications, certain facial features and profile characteristics are often prominent.

For example, this is a daguerreotype image with a subject whose features appear identical to the published photographs of Abraham Lincoln's copperhead (pro-Confederacy northerner) distracter Clement Vallandigham. William Stapp National Portrait Gallery, a quarter-plate daguerreotype with brass mat and half case, circa 1850s, rare.

A comparison between this daguerreotype with carte de visite of Clement Vallandigham with the preceding portrait on this page, and the identity of the man in the preceding photo is confirmed as Vallandigham. "E & H. T. Anthony," circa early 1860s, 2⅜" x 4", **$35-$50**.

Glued to the rear of the portrait at top is a 3⅞" x 1⅜" strip of paper identifying the engraving as being from a daguerreotype and the subject as Maj. Gen. Zachary Taylor. It also lists Taylor's Mexican-American war battles and his campaign slogan as Whig candidate for president—"General Taylor never surrenders."

BRASS-FRAMED PHOTOGRAPHS
Ferrotypes

With the 1860 election, photographic processes discovered and commercialized during the 1850s were used to revolutionize campaigning. Ferrotypes were glued to the indented centers of circular brass medals that already had their outer edges struck with the name of the candidate, the year and various wreath designs.

They frequently pictured the presidential candidate on one side and his running mate on the reverse. Campaign ferrotypes with candidates for president and vice president in the same picture (jugates) are rarer and considerably more valuable. As with traditional campaign medals, it wasn't unusual for the brass frames to have holes through which ribbon was threaded.

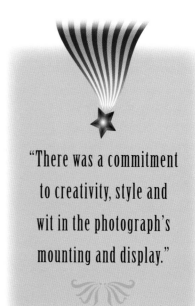

"There was a commitment to creativity, style and wit in the photograph's mounting and display."

Abraham Lincoln and Hannibal Hamlin, republican candidates, brass-framed ferrotype (front and back shown), 1860, 25 mm, **$300-$400**.

Sometimes ferrotypes were applied only to the non-pin sides of medals. George McClellan, democratic candidate for president, brass-framed ferrotype, 1864, 26 mm, **$200-$300**.

John Bell and Edward Everett, constitutional union candidates, brass-framed ferrotype (front and back shown), 1860, 25 mm, **$300-$400**.

Stephen Douglas and Herschel Johnson, northern democratic candidates, brass-framed ferrotype (front and back shown), 1860, 23 mm, **$300-$400**.

Left: John Breckinridge and Joseph Lane, southern democratic candidates, brass-framed ferrotype (front and back shown), 1860, 25 mm, **$300-$400**.

In some cases a ferrotype was simply enclosed with a brass frame and cardboard backing, with a pin through the top of the rear rim making it possible to wear. Illustrated are three ferrotypes of Civil War Union officers in uniform, all of whom also had presidential ambitions, **$150-$200** each.

This is a rare example of a large presidential ferrotype, Ulysses S. Grant, circa1870s-to-early-1880s, 5" x 6⅞".

George McClellan brass-framed ferrotype, "Abbott & Co.," circa 1861-'64, 1⅜" x 1⅝".

John Fremont brass-framed ferrotype, "Abbott & Co.," circa 1861-'64, 1⅜" x 1⅝".

Benjamin Butler brass-framed ferrotype, circa 1861-'64, 1⅜" x 1⅝".

Heavy gold-colored pot metal bug with pin in back for wearing, circa 1896-1900, 3½" x 3¾", **$30-$50**.

This is an interesting ferrotype because the young political activist is wearing a large metal "Gold/Silver Bug" on his jacket lapel and several smaller ones, circa 1896-1900, 2⅜" x 3⅛", **$100-$125**.

PAPER PHOTOGRAPHS

It was not until the late 1850s that glass negatives made it possible to produce large quantities of sharp, relatively inexpensive photographic copies, and just in time for the 1860 presidential election. As in the case of ferrotypes, paper photographs with cardboard backing were often simply outfitted with brass frames and pins for wearing.

Abraham Lincoln photo with brass frame, circa 1863-'64, 1" x 1¼", **$75-$100**.

Ulysses Grant photo with brass frame, circa 1860s, ¾" x 1", **$50-$75**.

Abraham Lincoln photo with brass frame attached to ribbon and held by eagle pin, circa 1863-'64, ¾" x 1", **$200-$250**.

"U.S. Grant," photo with brass frame, circa 1860s, ¾" x 1", **$50-$75**.

Andrew Johnson photo with brass frame, circa 1860s, ¾" x 1", **$50-$75**.

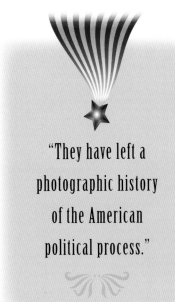

Although some ferrotype pins were still produced even during the 1880s, mass produced albumen paper photographs assumed greater popularity. The brass and copper shell frames that held political photographs during the 1870s and 1880s displayed a remarkable variety of designs, but usually with no embossing of any particular names of the subjects in the photos.

If there was identification of the subjects in the political photographs, and often there was not, the names were usually on the photos, not the frames. It was expected that the public in the past was familiar with the faces of the major candidates.

Each of the below photographs ranges in value from **$200-$300** each.

James Garfield ferrotype set in a brass shell frame with border of roses and heart-shaped extensions, 1880.

Rutherford Hayes photo in circular brass frame with a floral-like decorative border, 1876, 26 mm.

Grover Cleveland and Allen Thurman photos set in a decorative, shield-shaped, brass, shell frame and featuring an eagle pin clasp, 1888, 34 x 47 mm.

Horatio Seymour ferrotype set in a circular brass frame with borders of open loops, 23 mm.

Ulysses Grant ferrotype set in a brass six-pointed star frame pin, circa 1868, 29 x 32 mm.

Horatio Seymour ferrotype set in a circular satin-covered frame, 1868, 23 mm.

Samuel Tilden photo in circular brass frame showcasing a floral-like decorative border, 1876, 26 mm.

Rutherford Hayes and William Wheeler jugate photo featuring a red paper border in a circular brass frame pin, 1876, 25 mm, **$300-$400**.

Ulysses Grant photo set in white metal, flag-shaped frame pin, circa 1868, 24 x 32 mm.

Three Benjamin Harrison photos, two as adornments on lapel studs (1888, 18 mm and 26 mm) and one in a circular tin frame pin (circa 1892, 23 mm), **$35-$50** each.

James Blaine photo set in circular tin frame pin, circa 1884, 21 mm, **$35-$50**.

Grover Cleveland photo set in a lapel stud, 1884, 15 mm, **$25-$40**.

CARTE DE VISITE PHOTOGRAPHS

A carte de visite is a type of albumin photograph (or ferrotype) mounted on a 2½" x 4" card. Its political impact in the United States was mostly during the 1860s and early 1870s. Unlike daguerreotypes, celebrity pictures could be mass-produced for sale to collectors or campaign agents.

Today, a carte de visite of a presidential candidate would sell for **$25** to well over **$100** depending on the person, the condition, the rarity and the photographer. The imprint of the photographer was usually placed on the card's reverse. The value of the card might be inflated simply because the picture was taken by such famous American photographers as Charles D. Fredricks, Mathew Brady and Abraham Bogardus, or the major supplier and publishing firm, E. & H.T. Anthony.

Not infrequently, other photographers might make pirated copies for sale. The back side of the carte de visite would then probably be blank and the picture somewhat less than sharp. Such pirated copies might have been less costly, but they are desirable as contemporary collectibles.

John Fremont, 1856 republican candidate for president, circa 1860, **$20-$30**.

Gen. Winfield Scott, "E. & H. T. Anthony" from Brady negatives, circa 1860, **$35-$50**.

⭐ **Each of the following Abraham Lincoln carte de visite photographs is worth approximately $30-$50.**

Abraham Lincoln, "C. D. Fredricks & Co.," circa 1860s.

Abraham Lincoln, "Winder's Cartes de Visite Photographic Gallery," circa 1860s.

Abraham Lincoln, circa 1860s.

Abraham Lincoln photo on embossed card, "Salisbury, Bro. & Co./ Carte de Visites of all Noted Persons," circa 1860s.

⭐ **To follow are four Abraham Lincoln composite photographs, circa 1860s, $40-$60 each.**

Abraham Lincoln with key military members.

Abraham Lincoln with 41 top military personnel (photo without cardboard backing).

Abraham Lincoln with military "Peace Commissioners."

Abraham Lincoln with Cabinet members.

Shown above are four carte de visite photographs of Abraham Lincoln with his family, with only one of the photos—that of Lincoln sitting with his son—copied from an original. Mary Todd and Robert Lincoln were artistically added later. Obtaining an actual photo of Mary Todd standing with her husband would have required the invasive skills of the modern paparazzi, circa 1860s, **$30-$60** each.

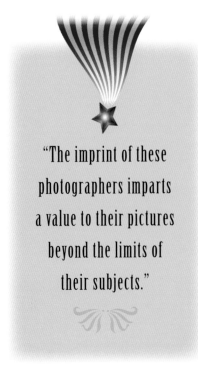

"The imprint of these photographers imparts a value to their pictures beyond the limits of their subjects."

Stephen Douglas standing, "E. Anthony," circa 1860, **$50-$75**.

S. A. Douglas, "Brady's National Photographic Portrait Galleries," circa 1860, **$50-$75**.

Jefferson Davis, circa 1860, **$50-$75**.

Stephen Douglas, "Case & Getchell," circa 1860-'62, **$50-$75**.

"Gen'l. Geo. B. McClellan," standing, 1864 democrat for president, "Brady/ E. Anthony," circa 1861, **$75-$125**.

George McClellan, circa 1861, **$25-$35**.

George Pendleton, Democratic Party vice president candidate in 1864, "C. D. Fredricks & Co.," circa 1860s, **$50-$75**.

Andrew Johnson seated, "Philada. Photographic Co.," circa 1860s, **$25-$40**.

Henry Wilson, 1872 republican for vice president, "C. D. Fredricks & Co.," circa 1870s, **$35-$50**.

Schuyler Colfax, 1868 republican for vice president, circa 1860s, **$20-$30**.

SCHUYLER COLFAX.

Andrew Johnson's Cabinet, including Secretary of War Stanton whose firing led to Johnson's House of Representative impeachment, circa 1860s., **$25-$40**.

PRESIDENT ANDREW JOHNSON.

Henry Wilson, "J.W. Black," circa 1870s, **$35-$50**.

Andrew Johnson, circa 1865-'68, **$25-$40**.

☆ Four Ulysses Grant photos, $50-$100 each:

"Lieut. Gen. U.S. Grant," with memorial ribbon hanging from his sleeve, circa 1860s.

Gen. Ulysses Grant, circa 1860s.

"Grant in Peace," photo of art work and great campaign item for a military candidate, circa 1860s.

Gen. Ulysses Grant and other top military, including Winfield Scott Hancock (top right), 1880 democrat for president, "E. & H. T. Anthony," circa 1860s.

Horace Greeley, circa 1870s, **$30-$40**.

Horace Greeley, 1872 democrat for president, "C. D. Fredricks & Co.," circa 1870s, **$75-$100**.

"Seymour and Blair," 1868 democratic team, circa 1868, **$50-$100**.

Horatio Seymour carte de visite with embossed card frame, "C. D. Fredricks & Co.," circa 1868, **$50-$100**.

"Grant Family," Ulysses Grant's wife was usually photographed from side view because she was cross-eyed, circa 1860s, **$35-$60**.

"Hon. Horace Greeley," side view, with reverse advertisement by jewelry wholesale dealer offering "Life Photographs of Greeley, Grant, and 100 other subjects given to every one buying $1.00 worth or more," circa 1870s, 2½" x 4⅛", **$50-$75**.

Horatio Seymour, 1868 democrat for president, "Gurney & Son," circa 1867-'68, **$50-$100**.

Lucretia Mott, anti-slavery and women's rights leader, circa 1860s-1870s, **$150-$250**.

Victoria Woodhull, circa 1870s, **$150-$250**.

Victoria Woodhull, suffragist and first woman to run for president (Equal Rights Party) in 1872, wearing hat, circa 1870s, **$150-$200**.

Rutherford B. Hayes, 1876 republican for president, circa 1870s, 2½" x 4⅛", **$40-$60**.

B. Gratz Brown, 1872 democrat for vice president, circa 1870s, **$30-$40**.

James Garfield, republican for president, circa 1880, **$30-$50**.

Samuel J. Tilden, democrat for president, "Warren's Portraits," circa 1876, 2½" x 4⅛", **$100-$125**.

James Garfield, circa 1880, 2½" x 4⅛", **$30-$50**.

President James Garfield, circa 1880-'81, **$30-$50**.

Two Civil War photos of Gen. Winfield Hancock, "J.E. Mc-Clees" and "Gurney & Son," circa 1860s, **$50-$75** each.

William A. Wheeler, 1876 republican for vice president, circa 1870s, **$40-$60**.

"President Garfield and Family," featuring individual photos of each person, circa 1880-'81.

"Gen. Chester A. Arthur, Rep. Candidate for Vice President 1880," **$35-$50**.

Winfield Hancock in suit, democrat for president, "Knecht," circa 1880, 2½" x 4⅛", **$50-$75**.

James Blaine, republican for president, circa 1884, 2½" x 4⅛", **$35-$50**.

Civil War photo of John Logan, 1884 republican for vice president, circa 1860s, **$30-$40**.

CABINET CARDS

Cabinet cards are photographs mounted to 4¼" x 6½" cards. From the mid-1870s to the 1890s, they were arguably the most popular photographic size. The photographers Mora, N.Y., Sarony, N.Y., and Gurney, N.Y., were particularly noted for their cabinet photographs of celebrities.

Ulysses Grant in civilian suit, 1868 republican for president, and Mrs. Ulysses Grant facing sideways, "Brady's National Photographic Portrait Galleries," circa 1860s, **$200-$300** for the pair.

"Gen. Ulysses S. Grant," circa 1870s, **$25-$40**.

Schuyler Colfax, 1868 republican for vice president, "Sarony & Co.," circa 1860s, **$75-$100**.

"Horace Greeley," 1872 democrat for president, "Sarony," circa 1870s, **$75-$100**.

Horace Greeley, "Pearsall," circa 1870s, **$75-$100**.

"President Hayes & Wife," elected president in 1876, "Ross," circa1870s, **$75-$100**.

Winfield Hancock facing left, "Pach," circa 1880, **$75-$100**.

Henry Wadsworth Longfellow and Peter Cooper, founder of Cooper Union and 1876 Greenback Party candidate for president, "Sarony," circa 1870s, **$75-$100**.

"Gen. Winfield S. Hancock, Democratic Candidate for President 1880," reverse has advertisement for Vaseline products, **$50-$75**.

James Garfield, republican for president, "E. E. Sawtelle," circa 1880, **$75-$100**.

Mrs. James Garfield, "E. E. Sawtelle," circa 1880, **$30-$40**.

James Garfield and Mrs. Garfield, "Litchfield," circa 1880, **$75-$100**.

Winfield Hancock, circa 1880, **$50-$75**.

James Garfield, circa 1880, **$30-$50**.

Grover Cleveland, democrat for president, 1884, **$25-$40**

President Grover Cleveland, circa 1885-'88, **$20-$30**.

Mrs. Grover Cleveland, circa 1880s, **$20-$30**.

Photo of three pictures of President Cleveland, his wife and baby, circa 1880s, **$25-$40**.

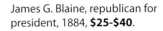

Allen Thurman, democratic candidate for vice president, 1888, **$25-$40**.

James G. Blaine, republican for president, 1884, **$25-$40**.

James G. Blaine, "Pach Bro's," circa 1880s, **$75-$100**.

James Blaine, reverse has department store advertisement, circa 1880s, **$25-$40**.

John A. Logan, republican for vice president, 1884, **$25-$40**.

Gen. Benjamin Harrison, republican for president, 1888, **$25-$40**.

"Benjamin Harrison/Levi P. Morton" and the slogan "We Are All Right," circa 1888, **$50-$75**.

Gen. Benjamin Harrison, circa 1888, **$25-$40**.

President Harrison with flag, which was likely applied later, and reverse advertising "Beecham's Pills," "London Stereoscopic & Photographic Co., Ltd.," circa 1889-'92, **$35-$50**.

"Benj. F. Butler," Greenback Party presidential candidate in 1884, circa 1880s, **$35-$50**.

Levi Morton, republican for vice president, 1888, **$25-$40**.

Benjamin. F.
Butler, "Warren,"
circa 1880s,
$75-$100.

WM. J. BRYAN AND FAMILY.

William Bryan, "Alfcamp,"
circa 1896-1900, **$50-$75**.

"Wm. J. Bryan and Family," with reverse advertisement for Vaseline products, circa 1900, **$20-$35**.

William McKinley, "Saybor's,"
circa 1896-1900, **$25-$40**.

WILLIAM McKINLEY.

William McKinley, standing,
circa 1896-1900, **$20-$30**.

International Art Publishing Co.,

William McKinley, "International Art Publishing Co.," circa 1896-1900, **$25-$40**.

GARRET A. HOBART.

Garret Hobart, republican for vice president, "Alfred S. Campbell," circa 1896, **$25-$40**.

Pictures larger than cabinet photographs were also made. These are just a few examples.

Ulysses Grant and Schuyler Colfax, republicans for president and vice president in 1868, 8" x 9⅛", **$75-$100** in this condition.

A beardless Abraham Lincoln, apparently a salt print in original oval frame with flag strip, and flag strip was likely added later, "Samuel Fassatt," circa late-1850s, 8" x 10" cut to fit frame, rare.

Winfield Hancock, "A. Bogardus," circa 1880, 5⅛" x 8" x ⅜", "Boudoir Portrait," **$75-$100**.

Scene of what appears to be a campaign parade about to begin with horse-drawn wagons, drummers, flag wavers and assorted supporters. One person, standing third from the left dons a hat with wording that ends in letters "land" (Grover Cleveland ?), "E. M. Johnson, Crown Point N. Y.," circa 1880s, 8⅜" x 5⅛", **$100-$150**.

Theodore Roosevelt campaign photograph, "Hillen's Studio," circa 1910s, 11" x 14⅛", **$100-$150**.

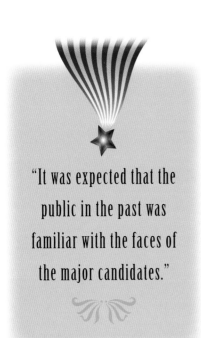

"It was expected that the public in the past was familiar with the faces of the major candidates."

"Cup Awarded For Best Decorations by Wilson-Marshall Club Of Lakewood (N. J.) Nov. 21, 1912," "Tezfast & Lets," 13⅛" x 11", **$50-$75**.

MICROPHOTOGRAPHS

Although commercial microphotography dates back to the 1850s, direct positive photos on glass slides were so small that one could only see them through a microscope. A political picture requiring a microscope would be an ineffective campaign tool, yet by the late-1860s the positive image was attached directly to a small cylindrical lens (Stanhope) for close, enlarged viewing. The lens could then be inserted within a ring, a carved piece of ivory, or any other small object.

Within the ivory "telescope" is a James Garfield memorial photograph of an engraving depicting the martyred president, seven family members and scenes of his life "from the cradle to the grave," circa 1881-'82, ¾", **$75-$100**.

Two metal pigs, each with a Stanhope lens in an opening through from the pig's tail and extending out its mouth. By looking through the pig's tail, one can see a photograph of Grover Cleveland or James G. Blaine. Each pig was undoubtedly shown by 1884 supporters of the opposite candidate, 1", **$100-$200** each.

Intricately carved letter opener and pen with Stanhope lens viewed though the top hole picturing Grover Cleveland and popular young wife Frances Folsom Cleveland, circa 1893-'96, 8⅞", **$100-$200**.

MECHANICAL PINS

The following are valued at **$200-$300** each unless otherwise noted.

When the presidential chair metal seat cover is down, it reveals the embossed question "The Presidential Chair. Who shall occupy it?" If a catch is released, the seat springs up revealing a photograph of Grover Cleveland or Benjamin Harrison. The first two Cleveland chairs on the left are slightly different, and the chair on the right is for Harrison, circa 1888, 1" x 2".

Republicans strongly supported a high tariff to protect American business from low-labor-cost, foreign competition. This is a miniature brass "G.O.P." elephant head that, when pulled open, reveals the image of locked lady's under garments and the words "For Protection," 1⅜" x 2½" held open.

The mechanical pin is a brass caricature of a formally dressed Grover Cleveland. By pressing the heel of his shoe, the arm and hand move out in a gesture of ridicule, circa 1880s, 1½" x I".

The gold bug symbolized the gold standard and William McKinley and Garret Hobart. The wings fold within the bug under spring pressure. Depressing the button at the tail end of the bug releases a catch and permits the wings to spring open, circa 1896, 1¼" x 1⅝" open.

Republican elephant with a metal blanket. When the catch is released, a hinged William McKinley and Garret Hobart picture is displayed, circa 1896, 1⅛" x 1⅛" open.

About three decades later, a similar piece was made depicting Warren Harding, but this piece also has a devil's tail emerge from the rear, circa 1920, 1⅝" l., **$100-$125**.

STEREO PHOTOGRAPHS

By using a two-lens camera and when viewed by a two-lens stereoscope, a pair of photographs provides a three dimensional image. Although stereographs existed during the daguerreotype period, their popularity increased significantly with paper photography.

Other than the first two cards, all cards shown are 3½" x 7". As time progressed, concave cards were produced to achieve what they believed to be a better stereo effect.

President Grant, his wife and son on the porch of his summer home, or "cottage by the sea," in Long Branch, N.J., "G. W. Pach," circa 1872, 3⅜" x 6⅞", **$20-$40**.

Election scene in Savannah, Ga., with large sign in front of crowd for republican Ulysses Grant, "J. N. Wilson," circa 1868, 3⅜" x 6⅞", **$15-$25**.

During the 1880s, non-stereo presidential pictures were sometimes given a three dimensional appearance by surrounding ordinary photos with dried-flower decorations, **$15-$25** each.

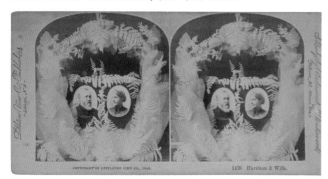

Benjamin Harrison and wife, Littleton View Co., circa 1888.

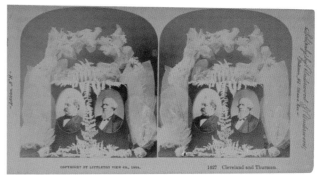

Grover Cleveland and Allen Thurman, Littleton View Co., circa 1888.

President and Mrs. William McKinley, Keystone View Co., circa 1897-1900.

Mr. and Mrs. William Bryan, Littleton View Co., circa 1896.

William McKinley and Gen. William Shafter in California, Keystone View Co., circa 1897-1900, **$15-$25**.

The mayor of Tuskegee, Ala., welcomes William McKinley, Strohmeyer & Wyman, circa 1899, **$15-$25**.

"During the first half of the 20th century, banquet cameras made it possible to develop large panoramic photographs."

William McKinley at his White House desk, Strohmeyer & Wyman, circa 1898, **$15-$25**.

William McKinley in White House cabinet room, Strohmeyer & Wyman, circa 1900, **$15-$25**.

William McKinley leaving church after addressing Civil War veterans, Pacific Grove, Ca., Underwood & Underwood, circa 1897-1901, **$15-$25**.

Theodore Roosevelt before a Noblesville, Ind., crowd , Keystone View Co., circa 1901-'04, **$15-$25**.

Roosevelt's "Western Tour-Speaking at Evanston, Ill.," R. Y. Young, circa 1903, **$15-$25**.

Roosevelt "Bowing to Admiring Throngs, Phila., Pa.," The Cosmos Series, circa 1901-'04, **$15-$25**.

Roosevelt in regular session with Cabinet, Underwood & Underwood, circa 1908, **$15-$25**.

Roosevelt in the White House Cabinet Room, H. C. White Co., circa 1901-'08, **$15-$25**.

Roosevelt signing bills, Underwood & Underwood, circa 1903, **$15-$25**.

William H. Taft at his desk, before he was president, Underwood & Underwood, circa 1906, **$10-$20**.

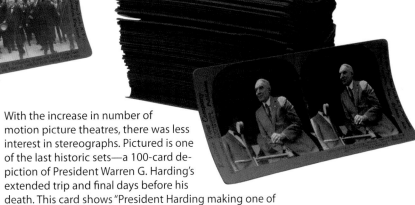

By the early 1900s, most middle class homes likely had a stereoscope and a large selection of stereographs. This picture, from a three-box set holding 300 World War I stereographs, shows Woodrow Wilson leaving Versailles Palace after signing the Peace Treaty, Keystone View Co., circa late 1910s, **$800-$1,000** for the set. A separate "book" held the stereoscope.

With the increase in number of motion picture theatres, there was less interest in stereographs. Pictured is one of the last historic sets—a 100-card depiction of President Warren G. Harding's extended trip and final days before his death. This card shows "President Harding making one of his first speeches on his Alaskan trip … ," Keystone View Co., circa 1923, **$15-$25** each card or **$800-$1,000** for the set.

GLASS PLATES

Theodore Roosevelt's Rough Rider heroics and those of other Spanish American War heroes were dramatized with glass slides. This set includes 48 photographic lantern slides, with the slide that is outside the box showing Roosevelt, circa 1899-1900, 1½" x 6⅛", **$100-$150** for the set.

During the 1920s, political glass slides were used to project candidates on theater screens or building walls, "Standard Slide Corp.," 3¼" x 4", **$35-$50** each slide. They include: Alfred E. Smith for President, circa 1928; Herbert Hoover for President, circa 1928; Warren Harding for President/ Calvin Coolidge for Vice President, circa 1920; Calvin Coolidge for President, Charles Dawes for Vice President, circa 1924; Charles Curtis for Vice President, circa 1928; and Robert Lafollette for President/ Burton Wheeler for Vice President, circa 1924.

PANORAMIC PHOTOGRAPHS

During the first half of the 20th century, banquet cameras made it possible to develop large panoramic photographs. These were particularly useful in portraying a long line of people or a convention hall filled with thousands of delegates.

Herbert Hoover is the front-center subject of this framed panoramic photo, circa 1929-'32, 7" x 17¾", **$30-$50**.

Townsend National Convention panoramic photo, Taylor Photographers, 1940, 8" x 35¾", **$50-$75**.

PHOTOMONTAGE

Photo advertisement card displaying 27 famous people including James Garfield in the center and James Blaine on the lower left , "Abraham Bogardus," circa 1880, 3¼" x 4⅞", rare.

Photomontage blending dozens of negatives to produce multiple-image photographs of William Bryan, Underwood & Underwood, circa 1908, 6⅞" x 10⅞ ", **$75-$100** each.

Thomas Dewey photomontage combining three pictures showing him drinking, smoking and thinking, International News, circa 1940s, 6⅝" x 8½", **$20-$30**.

PRIVATE ALBUMS

From Nov. 18, 1928, to Jan. 7, 1929, the *U.S.S. Utah's* mission was to pick up President Herbert Hoover and his wife from a diplomatic "good will" trip to South America. Enclosed in this leather-bound album are hundreds of photos of the crew's daily activities, as well as pictures of the President and a menu card signed by Hoover and his wife, circa 1928-'29, 8¾" x 13⅞", **$1,000-$2,500**.

President Herbert Hoover and his wife aboard *U.S.S. Utah*, 2¾" x 4½".

U.S.S. Utah menu signed by President Herbert Hoover and his wife, 5" x 7". The *U.S.S. Utah* was later sunk by the Japanese at Pearl Harbor.

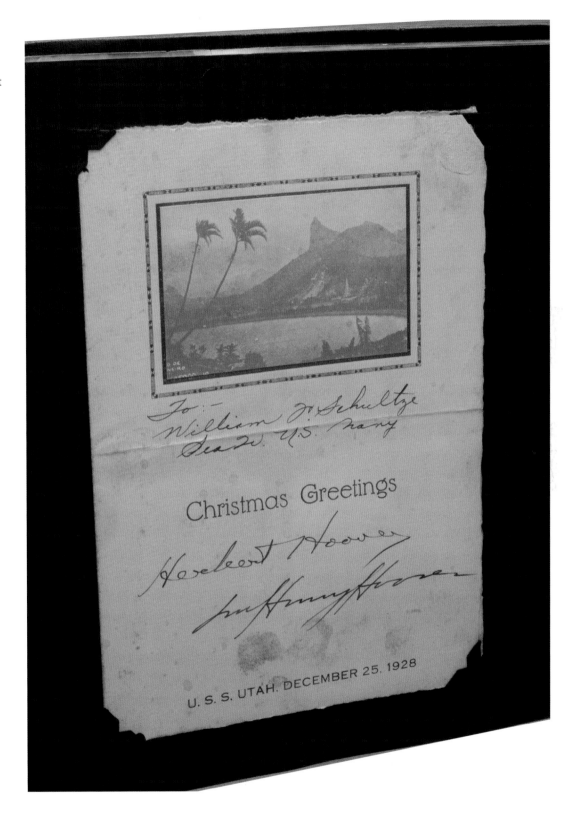

COATTAIL PHOTOGRAPHS

When a candidate for local or state office is photographed with the president or contender for the presidency, there is a mutual advantage. For the local candidates it is an impressive sign of their connections and influence.

Campaign photograph of John F. Kennedy with congressional candidate Jack Dunn, circa 1960, 30" x 40", **$100-$150**.

Framed campaign photograph of President Eisenhower with New York congressional candidate Julius Reinlieb, circa 1956, 25¼" x 37¼", **$75-$100**.

Photograph of Lyndon Johnson and Dean Rusk, circa 1960s, 15½" x 19¾", **$25-$40**. Johnson had a full-time staff member who took hundreds of thousands of photos of Johnson with other individuals. The other individual would be expected to display the picture prominently in his office, reinforcing his loyalty and support for Johnson.

MAGAZINE AND NEWSPAPER PHOTOGRAPHS

The backs of magazine and newspaper photos usually identified the picture's significance and gave photo credits, **$30-$50** each.

President Franklin Delano Roosevelt on the eve of his 62nd birthday, Harris & Ewing, Jan. 29, 1944, 6⅝" x 8½".

Franklin Delano Roosevelt signing a law, "Wired Photo-Wide World," circa 1940, 8⅛" x 9⅞".

Franklin Delano Roosevelt and 4-H campers, "Wide World Photos," 1940, 7" x 9".

Franklin Delano Roosevelt visits first army maneuvers, "Wide World Photos," August 1940, 9" x 7⅛".

AUTOGRAPHED PHOTOS

Republican presidential candidate (1944 and 1948) Thomas Dewey signed campaign photo, 1939, 7⅞" x 9⅞", **$125-$200**.

Democratic candidate (1952) for vice president, John Sparkman signed photograph, circa 1950s, 7⅝" x 10⅛", **$50-$75**.

President Warren Harding photograph in its original frame, circa 1920, 23¼" x 27½", rare.

Signed photograph of Vice President John Garner, Harris & Ewing, circa 1930s, 7½" x 10¼", **$50-$75**.

Official White House photo signed by Gerald Ford, circa 1973-'76, 13⅞" x 18", **$75-$100**.

Joseph Cannon, speaker of the House and presidential hopeful, signed photograph in its original frame, circa 1917, 13¼" x 16¼", **$75-$100**.

Official White House photo signed by Richard Nixon, circa 1969-'74, 13½" x 17½", **$75-$100**.

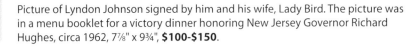

Picture of Lyndon Johnson signed by him and his wife, Lady Bird. The picture was in a menu booklet for a victory dinner honoring New Jersey Governor Richard Hughes, circa 1962, 7⅞" x 9¾", **$100-$150**.

PRINTING PLATES

Before and after World War I, *Harvey's Weekly* was an anti-Woodrow Wilson, pro-republican magazine that used zinc printing plates for creative and humorous cartoons. Copper plates were for half-tone photographic prints.

"Elect Kennedy and Johnson" embossed non-metallic printing plate, "Coak—Drawn for the AFL-CIO News," circa 1960, 6⅞" x 7⅝", **$20-$35**.

Printed photograph of "Calvin Coolidge/ Republican Nominee for Vice-President," *Harvey's Weekly,* June 19, 1920, Vol. 3 No. 25, p. 5, 8½" x 12", **$15-$25**.

The actual copper plate attached to wood used to print the preceding Calvin Coolidge picture, circa 1920, 7½" x 10⅛", rare.

VIDEOTAPE

Modern political campaign headquarters and pressure groups likely distribute DVDs across the country, but up until recently videotapes were the preferred film format.

This is an example of a political videotape ridiculing Vice President Dan Quayle. "The Unofficial Dan Quayle Video," "Video Treasures," circa 1992, 4⅛" x 7⅜", **$10-$15**.

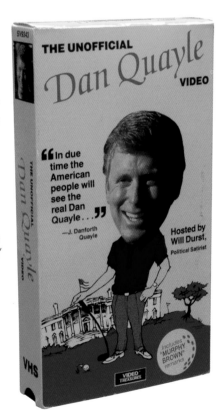

3

★★★★★

BUTTONS, TABS, FLASHERS

and

SYMBOLIC ITEMS, 1896 TO 1964

★★★★★★★★

PARKER-DAVIS

I t was not until the 1896 presidential election that companies employed transparent celluloid to seal photographs or prints. The Whitehead and Hoag Co. of Newark, N.J., was one of the earliest and most famous button, badge and medal manufacturers to seal buttons with celluloid. With its 1896 patent of the celluloid button process, there was a clear movement away from the manufacturing of more expensive medals and tokens.

In the following photos, when buttons are shown in groups, the value ranges given are for the majority of the pieces displayed. The more rare pins in each group setting could fetch higher values, some hundreds of dollars apiece. 🌿

Rare.

Photography for miniature campaign pieces went through a transition period during the 1896 and 1900 elections. Many varieties of badges were made, combining old and new techniques. These badges and buttons illustrate the variations, **$40-$150** each.

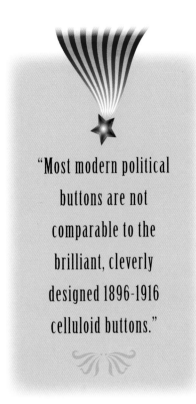

Although expensively made buttons, pins and badges were nice looking, the celluloid campaign button rapidly overtook and virtually eliminated the production of traditional and early experimental pieces. Except for very limited production items, most modern political buttons are not comparable to the brilliant, beautifully colored and cleverly designed celluloid items of the 1896-1916 elections.

After World War I, campaign buttons lost their brilliant, colorful designs. They tended to be black half-tone prints or photographs. Often, companies disregarded celluloid and simply produced pictures lithographed to sheet metal and pressed into button shape.

Ironically, the rather dull, colorless buttons, particularly touting democratic candidates of the 1920 and 1924 elections, include some of the rarest and most valuable pieces. Even 40 years ago, they were difficult to obtain, and now most auction for 20 or 30 times their cost during the 1960s.

Values are usually highest for jugates, picturing presidential and vice-presidential candidates in the same images, worth less when only one candidate is pictured and still lower when words only are depicted.

Particularly attractive pieces, interesting or unusual button designs and buttons larger than the usual ⅞" or 1¼" sizes, are highest priced in their category ranges. Some of the rare items are denoted as such.

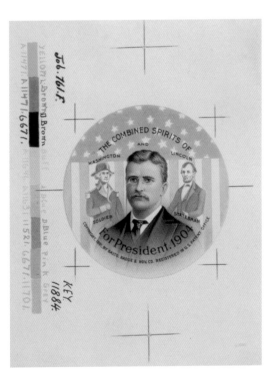

The Theodore Roosevelt print is a conceptual button and illustrates the many different colors used to give the picture its beauty, "Balto. Badge & Nov. Co.," circa 1901-'04, 3½" x 5", rare.

William McKinley-related buttons and pins, 1896 and 1900, **$20-$75** each, with some of the rare and jugate (showing both candidates for president and vice president) pieces valued at **$100-$300** apiece.

"Values are often highest for jugates, picturing presidential and vice-presidential candidates in the same images."

"After World War I, campaign buttons lost their brilliant, colorful designs."

William Jennings Bryan-related buttons, pins and badges, 1896, 1900 and 1908 election periods, **$20-$75** each. The "No Cross of Gold/ No Crown of Thorns" button refers to Bryan's convention speech and is valued at **$100-$125**, as are most jugates. Notice the use of similar designs, but in a variety of sizes, with the larger the button size, the higher its value.

The 1904 Theodore Roosevelt pins, medals and buttons range in price from **$35-$125** each. Roosevelt was associated and identified through several symbols, including the Teddy Bear, the bull moose (in 1912) and the Rough Riders, with most of the latter buttons featuring him in uniform and his Rough Rider hat. The Rough Rider pin that depicts him on horseback would be in the **$600-$800** range. Some of the rare pins showing two or three candidates are valued at **$100-$300** apiece.

Rare.

Alton Parker-related buttons and pins, 1904, **$35-$100** each, with some of the jugates fetching **$150-$300** apiece.

A selection of William H. Taft pins, buttons and badges, 1908 and 1912 election years, **$10-$80** each, with some of the more rare jugates worth **$100-$200** apiece.

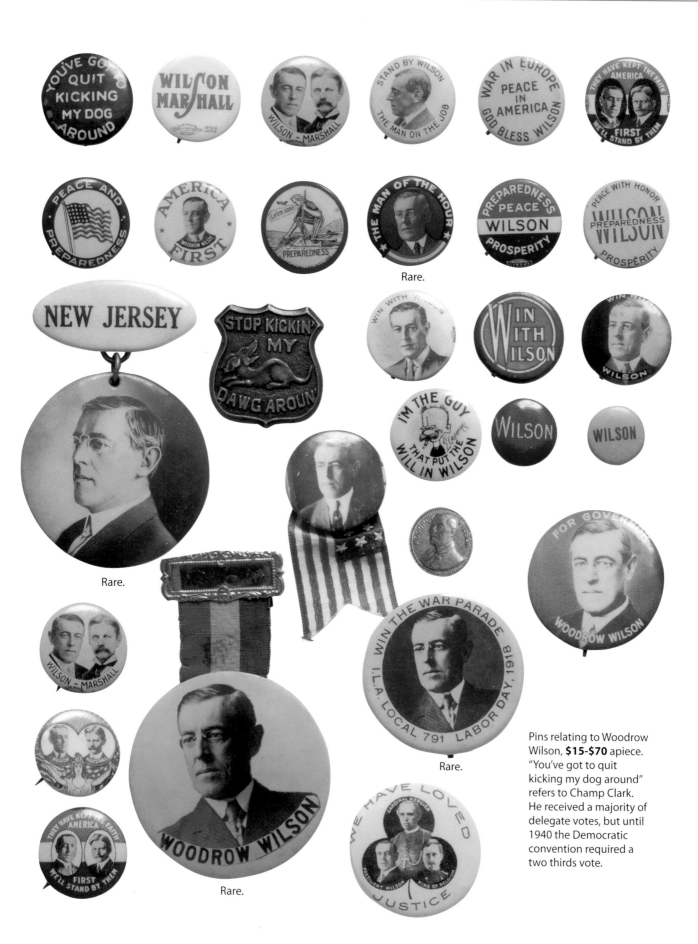

Rare.

Rare.

Rare.

Rare.

Rare.

Pins relating to Woodrow Wilson, **$15-$70** apiece. "You've got to quit kicking my dog around" refers to Champ Clark. He received a majority of delegate votes, but until 1940 the Democratic convention required a two thirds vote.

Charles E. Hughes buttons and badges, 1916, **$15-$80** each, with the four-leaf clover button valued at **$250-$300**; and the flag button with the word "Hughes" across the candidates chest (top left) reaching the **$150-$200** range.

Warren G. Harding buttons, 1920, **$10-$50** each.

James M. Cox buttons and pins, 1920, **$30-$200** each.

Robert La Follette buttons, 1924, **$20-$60** each.

Calvin Coolidge buttons and pins, 1924, **$10-$70** and up to **$100** each.

Herbert Hoover pins, buttons
and badges, 1928 and 1932,
$15-$75 each.

Rare.

Alfred E. Smith pins, badges and buttons, 1928, **$15-$60,** with some of the more rare jugate pins reaching **$200-$250** apiece. A cloth hat hangs from one Smith pin, **$40-$60**, and the other "hat pins" are plastic or metal, **$10-$15** each. Even an Al Smith donkey wears a hat, **$25-$35**.

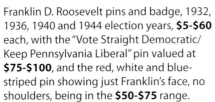

Franklin D. Roosevelt pins and badge, 1932, 1936, 1940 and 1944 election years, **$5-$60** each, with the "Vote Straight Democratic/ Keep Pennsylvania Liberal" pin valued at **$75-$100**, and the red, white and blue-striped pin showing just Franklin's face, no shoulders, being in the **$50-$75** range.

Nine-inch Franklin D. Roosevelt button, **$100-$150**.

Franklin D. Roosevelt pins and badges, 1932, 1936, 1940 and 1944 election years, **$5-$60** each. The Roosevelt-Harry Truman jugate (the sepia-tone button picturing both candidates), 1944, **$300-$400**; the "Vote For Roosevelt/ Guffey" pin, showing both candidates, **$200-$250**; and the button with ribbon that reads "Inauguration President Franklin D. Roosevelt, Washington, D.C., Jan. 20, 1937, **$50-$100**.

Above: Rare nine-inch Thomas Dewey button showing the then-governor candidate and fellow Republican candidates.

Thomas Dewey-related buttons, pins and badges, 1944 and 1948 elections, **$5-$70** each, with the "Dewey/ Bricker" jugate valued at **$100-$150**.

Nine-inch Harry S. Truman button, 1948, **$350-$500**.

Harry S. Truman buttons, 1948, **$25-$75** each, with some of the more rare pieces fetching **$100-$350** apiece.

Rare.

Henry Wallace buttons, 1948, **$15-$40** each.

Rare.

Alf Landon buttons, 1936, **$10-$60** each, with the "Sunflower Chain Club" button with felt sunflower backing valued at **$250-$300**, and the red, white and blue "jugate", **$75-$100**.

Rare.

Rare.

Dwight D. Eisenhower buttons and pins, 1952 and 1956 election years, **$5-$50 e**ach, with some of the more rare Eisenhower/ Richard Nixon jugates fetching **$75-$450** each, and the "Time For A Change" button with the baby in "I Like IKE" diapers, **$450-$550**.

Rare.

Rare.

Rare.

Rare

Adlai Stevenson buttons, pins and badges, 1952 and 1956 election years, **$5-$50** each, with jugates being **$50-$125**.

John F. Kennedy buttons and pins, 1960, **$10-$75** each.

Rare cardboard.

Richard Nixon buttons, 1960, **$5-$40** each.

Pro-Lyndon Johnson and anti-Barry Goldwater buttons and pins, 1964, **$5-$50** each, with the "What — Me Worry?" pin valued at **$300-$400**. NJ Young Citizens, **$50-$100**.

Barry Goldwater buttons and pins, 1964, **$5-$25** each.

FLASHERS

When flashers are rotated and the viewing angles change, the pictures or words on the flashers change. These were popular attention grabbers during the 1950s and 1960s, **$10-$30**.

POLITICAL ISSUES

Space does not permit coverage of every political issue, or hot topic of the day, or minor party collectible, but the following photos illustrate two early campaign issues.

Women's suffrage buttons, circa 1910-'20, **$25-$50** each.

Pro-prohibition buttons and pins, circa 1900-'20, **$10-$50** each.

4

★ ★ ★ ★ ★

TEXTILES
and
CLOTHING
★ ★ ★ ★ ★ ★ ★ ★ ★

RIBBONS

Ribbons were some of the earliest campaign pieces to be worn pinned to clothing. They were clear and immediate expressions of partisans' political support. Even with increased use of photography, ribbons remained popular throughout the 19th and into the 20th centuries.

Usually, the candidates' pictures and/or campaign slogans were printed directly on the ribbons. Here are some examples.

Grover Cleveland "For President" multicolor ribbon with his image, 1884, 2" x 5⅜", **$50-$75**.

Youth's Temperance Society ribbon showing young man and woman in favor of water, 1840, 2⅜" x 4½", **$30-$50**.

William Henry Harrison, New England Convention ribbon with Harrison image and symbols of the New England Convention states, 1840, 2¾" x 5¾", **$100-$150**.

Henry Clay ribbon with his image, 1844, 2⅞" x 8⅜", **$100-$150**.

James Garfield and Chester Arthur narrow white ribbon, circa 1880, **$20-$30**.

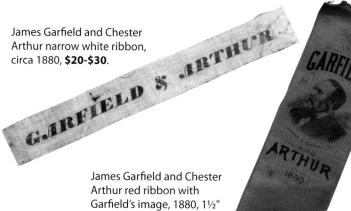

James Garfield and Chester Arthur red ribbon with Garfield's image, 1880, 1½" x 5¼", **$35-$50**.

Grover Cleveland and Thomas Hendricks ribbon featuring their images, Schweizer & J. Kartz, circa 1884, 1⅞" x 4¾", **$50-$75**.

James Blaine detailed image on a large silk, circa 1884, 6" x 5½", **$50-$75**.

Ribbons often included references to businesses and outside supporters, such as this "Real Estate And Land Owners/ McKinley And Hobart/ Sound Money" gold ribbon, circa 1896, 2¾" x 7", **$35-$50**.

Benjamin Harrison and Whitelaw Reid ribbon listing them and other republican candidates, including a poem urging a protective tariff, 1892, 2¼" x 7", **$40-$60**.

Three William Bryan ribbons, including a "Bryan 16=1" narrow white ribbon, circa 1896-1900, 1⅛" x 8½", **$20-$30**; a "Bryan and Sewall" ribbon of a 13-star U.S. flag, circa 1908, 2⅝" x 4⅞", **$40-$60**; and a W. J. Bryan red ribbon issued for the Cleveland Reception Committee, circa 1896-1908, **$30-$50**.

"Machinery, Railway Supply And Metal Assoc'n/ McKinley And Hobart/ New York City," Whitehead & Hoag Co., 1896, blue ribbon with red, white and blue flag attached, 2" x 5", **$35-$50**.

The Theodore Roosevelt picture ribbon was actually woven on a jacquard loom, "National Ribbon Company," circa 1901-'12, 3" x 5½", **$50-$75**.

Jacquard-woven ribbon picturing Theodore Roosevelt in his Cabinet office, circa 1901-'08, 5½" by 9½", **$75-$125**.

R.B. Hayes and W.A. Wheeler jacquard-loom-woven political picture ribbon, "B.B Tilt & Son," circa 1876, 2⅛" x 4⅜", **$100-$150**.

Benjamin Harrison and Whitelaw Reid badge with celluloid Harrison picture and Frelinghuysen Lancers ribbon, Whitehead & Hoag Co., 1892, 2¾" x 7½", **$100-$125**.

"Harrison & Morton/ Banking, Insurance & Real Estate Club" ribbon including celluloid picture of Harrison, Whitehead & Clark, circa 1888, 2¾" x 8½", **$100-$150**.

Harrison celluloid picture badge with red, white and blue ribbon and a 1⅜" x 1½" celluloid reading "Frelinghuysen Lancers, Newark, N.J.," Whitehead & Hoag Co., circa 1892, 2¾" x 9", **$100-$125**.

National Association of Democratic Clubs Convention celluloid with pictures of Grover Cleveland and Adlai Stevenson, attached to a light blue ribbon with red, white and blue flag and ¾-inch-diameter celluloid disk of Jefferson, 1892, 2½" x 4¾", **$100-$150**.

"Ribbons were clear
and immediate
expressions of partisans'
political support."

Sometimes photos were pasted directly onto ribbons.

Grover Cleveland and Thomas Hendricks photos on ribbon, "Brown & Sanson," circa 1884, 2½" x 5¾", **$75-$100**.

Ribbon urging Adlai Stevenson to select Senator John Kennedy as running mate, but the choice was given to convention delegates who chose Carey Kefauver, 1956, 2½" x 9½", **$100-$200**.

James Blaine and John Logan photos on ribbon, circa 1884, "Brown & Sanson," 2½" x 5¾", **$75-$100**.

Ribbon and button combinations were also popular. Each of the following three ribbons include 1¾", brass-framed celluloid pictures, Whitehead & Hoag Co., **$100-$150** each.

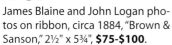

"McKinley & Roosevelt" picture badge ribbon, 1900, 2⅞" x 4⅞".

"McKinley & Hobart Club" picture badge ribbon, circa 1896, 2⅞" x 8½".

William McKinley and Garret Hobart picture badge with ribbon reading in part "Protection/ Reciprocity/ Sound Money," circa 1896, 2⅞" x 8½".

Alf Landon and Frank Knox yellow ribbons attached to a fabric sunflower with pin, 1936, 7½", **$20-$30**.

"Our Vice-President/ Guthrie/ Aug. 31, 1910" red, white and blue ribbon including 2-inch celluloid button of Vice President James Sherman (probably visiting the original Oklahoma capitol building), 4⅜", **$25-$35**.

"Prohibition and Reform," red ribbon with photos of John St. John and William Daniel, circa1884, 2" x 6", **$150-$200**.

Paper ribbon picturing William McKinley and Alex Crow, Jr., local Pennsylvanian, *The Philadelphia Inquirer*, 1896, 3" x 7⅜", **$25-$35**.

"Democratic Party Worker" paper ribbon picturing Al Smith, 1928, 2½" x 6¼", **$25-$35**.

Bayonne City Democratic Club ribbon for Woodrow Wilson's inauguration as New Jersey governor, January 17, 1911, 2⅛" x 5", rare.

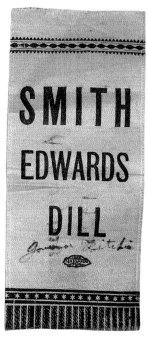

New Jersey ribbon for Alfred Smith with what appears to be Governor Ritchie's signature on front and "Aug. 25, 1928" on reverse, 2⅜" x 5¼", rare.

LAPEL BUTTONHOLE STUDS

In the late 1880s, gentlemen wore buttons covered in woven cloth touting political ideas and initiatives, as well as the names of political candidates. The buttons looked quite fashionable poking through lapel buttonholes.

The seven 1888 woven-cloth-covered studs and 1889 cloth-rim stud each measure ¾" and are valued at **$25-$40** apiece. They include a "Democratic Tariff Reform/ C&T (Cleveland and Thurman)" button; an "F.A. Potts Harrison & Morton Club" stud; a "Harrison & Morton Club" button; a "Republican Club/ OE" stud attached to an enameled "H&M" (Harrison & Morton) brass pin; a "Free Trade/ Free Land/ Free Men" pin with the image of a cat, circa 1880s; two "Harrison" buttons on woven U.S. flags; and a copper medal with a cloth rim, including the profile images of Benjamin Harrison and Whitelaw Reid, 1892.

BANDANAS AND SCARVES

Winfield Hancock and William English portrait bandana including historic scenes and symbols, "Hugh McCrossan," circa 1880, 17⅝" square, **$250-$400**.

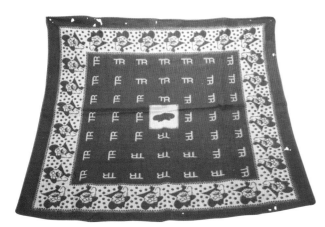

Theodore Roosevelt red and brown bandana with images of Roosevelt around the border, rows of "TR" and a red Rough Rider hat in the center, circa 1900-'04, 19¼" x 20½", **$50-$75**.

Grover Cleveland and Adlai Stevenson red and dark-blue bandana showcasing the image of a shield emphasizing "Tariff Reform," circa 1892-'96, 21½" x 26", **$100-$150**. Democrats strongly opposed the protective tariff.

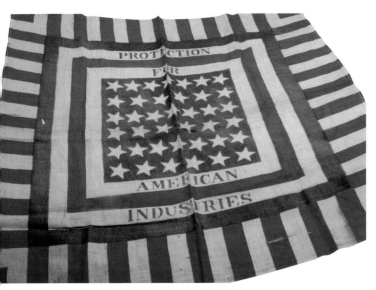

Benjamin Harrison red and gray banner showcasing the general's portrait surrounded by flags, an eagle, log cabin and Civil War scenes, circa 1888, 20¾" x 24¾", rare.

"Protection for American Industries" red and blue bandana with 39 stars in the center, circa late 1880s, 21¾" x 23¾", **$100**.

"Win With IKE For President/ I Like IKE" red and black Eisenhower portrait bandana, circa 1952-'56, 26" square, **$75-$100**.

Grover Cleveland portrait bandana, circa 1880s, 21½" x 25¼" framed, rare.

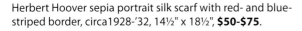

Herbert Hoover sepia portrait silk scarf with red- and blue-striped border, circa1928-'32, 14½" x 18½", **$50-$75**.

Louisiana Purchase Exposition, 1904, embroidered and printed silk souvenir picturing Theodore Roosevelt, 10" square, **$75-$125**.

PENNANTS

Franklin Roosevelt felt portrait pennant, circa mid-1930s-1940, 10¾" x 27¾", **$30-$50**.

"March 4 1933 Franklin D. Roosevelt Inauguration/ Washington D.C." felt pennant with sawn-wood Roosevelt image, 11½" x 27½", **$50-$75**.

"Elect Thomas E. Dewey President" felt portrait pennant, circa 1944-'48, 11¼" x 29", **$25-$40**.

Two John F. Kennedy felt pennants with photos, 11⅞" x 29¾" and 6⅞" x 17¾", circa 1961-'62, **$20-$25** each.

Three Dwight D. Eisenhower felt portrait pennants, **$25-$40** each, including "We Still Like IKE," 1956, 11½" x 29¾"; Washington D.C. Inauguration, Jan. 20, 1953, 11¾" x 29¼"; and Inauguration Jan. 20, 1953, with the images of Eisenhower and an elephant, 5¼" x 16¾".

"Vote Goldwater" felt pennant with photo, 1964, 11¾" x 30¾", **$25-$35**.

"Vote Democrat" felt pennant with die-cut opening to frame picture of Hubert Humphrey and Edmund Muskie, 1968, 8¾" x 19⅝", **$15-$20**.

"Welcome Muskie" felt pennant picturing a running donkey, circa 1968-'72, 8⅞" x 23¾", **$10-$15**.

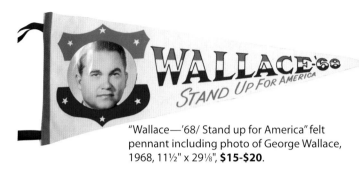

"Wallace—'68/ Stand up for America" felt pennant including photo of George Wallace, 1968, 11½" x 29⅛", **$15-$20**.

"Jimmy Carter/ The Next President Of The U.S.A/ 1976" felt pennant with image of Carter and U.S. flag, 1976, 8⅞" x 26½", **$15-$20**.

Three Richard Nixon felt pennants, two touting "Nixon's The One," 11⅞" x 29⅛" and 7" x 17¾", with pictures of Nixon; and the other "Vote Republican," 8¾" x 19⅝", with a picture of Nixon and Spiro Agnew, 1968-'72, **$15-$20** each.

BANNERS

Franklin Roosevelt image on yellow-tasseled banner, circa 1933-'40, 13½" x 21", **$40-$50**.

"Win With Franklin D. Roosevelt Our Next President" red, white and blue portrait banner, circa 1936-'40, 9" x 11⅞ ", **$40-$50**.

"We Need You F.D.R./ God Bless America" red, white and blue Franklin Roosevelt portrait banner with "Equality/Liberty/ Justice" beneath picture, circa 1936-'40, 9" x 11½", **$40-$50**.

Far left: "God Bless America/ Wendell Willkie/ Our Next President" red, white and blue portrait banner, circa 1940, 4⅞" x 6⅜", **$40-$50**.

"To Keep The Nation Firm/ Give Him Another Term" red, white and blue Franklin Roosevelt portrait banner, circa 1936-'40, 4¾" x 6⅜", **$40-$50**.

Two Roosevelt picture banners: "Roosevelt For President" and "A Gallant Leader," circa 1930s, 38¾" x 59" each, **$75-$100** apiece.

"For a Square Deal/ Win With Willkie/ Vote Republican" red, white and blue Wendell Willkie portrait banner with "Freedom/ Unity/ Defense/ Economy" beneath picture, circa 1940, 7¾" x 11⅛", **$40-$50**.

TAPESTRIES

William Taft woven tapestry showing close connection to his predecessor and key supporter Theodore Roosevelt, circa 1908, 4' x 4', rare.

Numerous tapestries were imported during the John F. Kennedy candidacy, presidency and memorial. The tapestry portrays him and a World War II PT boat, circa 1960, 20¼" x 37¾", **$30-$50**.

HANDKERCHIEFS

"I Like IKE" and "I Say Adlai" embroidered handkerchiefs, circa 1952-'56, one of which is 10½" square and the other 10¾" x 11", **$15-$25** each; and an embroidered "Goldwater '64" folded linen on a sheet of plastic, 1964, 3⅜" x 4⅞", **$10-$15**. The latter is a faux handkerchief for the purpose of wearing in the top pocket of a suit jacket where the words will be seen.

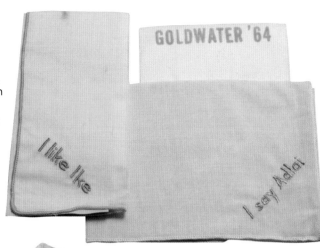

Alfred Smith cotton handkerchief with his image, circa 1928, 11½" x 11¼", **$35-$50**; a Herbert Hoover cotton handkerchief, circa 1928, 11½" x 11¼", **$35-$50**; and a William McKinley and Garret Hobart handkerchief picturing the candidates, a patriotic design and words urging "Protection" and "Sound Money," 1896, 17¼" x 17½", **$50-$75**.

DITTY BAG

Woodrow Wilson patriotic ditty bag with Wilson's image, metallic embroidery, flags and the words "For Our Flag And Country," circa 1916-'20, 9½" x 10½", **$35-$50**.

SMALL FLAGS

"Theiss' New Music Hall" cloth touting Grover Cleveland and New York candidates for governor and mayor, and attached to the back of a 38-star U. S. flag, circa 1888, 1⅜" x 2¾", **$40-$50**.

"Harrison And Morton" woven, 30-star U. S. flag, circa 1888, 2¼" x 4", **$40-$50**.

Alf Landon and Frank Knox brown-on-yellow flag attached to wooden rod, circa 1936, 3⅜" x 5", **$30-$40**.

"Votes For Women" brown on yellow flag attached to wooden rod, circa 1910s, 5¾" x 9⅝", **$35-$50**; and a "Votes For Women" brown-on-yellow felt pennant, circa 1910s, 1½" x 5", **$25-$40**.

WOOL SASH

"Willkie for President" printed on red, white and blue flag, circa 1940, 4" x 5¾", **$15-$20**.

"Votes For Women" felt sash, circa 1910s, 1½" x 24", **$50-$75**.

ARMBAND

"Landon-Knox" yellow felt armband, circa 1936, 3⅜" x 8¾", **$35-$50**.

PILLOWS AND CUSHIONS

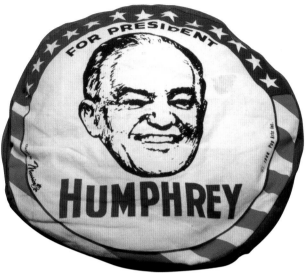

"Win With Willkie" dark-blue, woven cushion in support of Wendell Willkie with words repeated throughout the design, circa 1940, 12" square, **$30-$50**.

Hubert Humphrey for president, red, white and blue cushion with the candidate's image, "Maurice/ Pop Arts Inc.," 1968, 14" diameter, **$20-$30**.

HATS

Prior to the 1960s, at a time when hats were a more-common part of people's daily attire, hat styles were often associated with specific candidates who either wore them or personified such hats. Political activists, in turn, wore campaign hats in support of their favorite candidates.

During the 1930s and early 1940s, it was popular for young boys to wear cut-felt beanies covered completely with pins, and often campaign buttons. The value depends on the display, quality and condition.

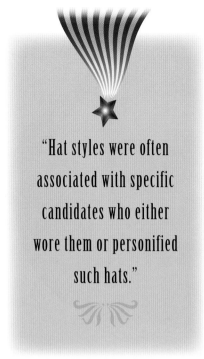

"Hat styles were often associated with specific candidates who either wore them or personified such hats."

"G.O.P. /Barry Goldwater" plastic hat with picture sticker applied to front, 1964, **$10-$15**; and Lyndon Johnson plastic cowboy hat with picture sticker applied to front, 1964, **$10-$20**.

"L.B.J. For The U.S.A." plastic hat with paper picture wrap, 1964, **$10-$15** and "L.B.J. for the U.S.A." lady's straw hat with ribbon wrapped around the side, 1964, **$10-$20**.

"Harry S. Truman For President" felt beanie with embossed face on top, **$75-$100**.

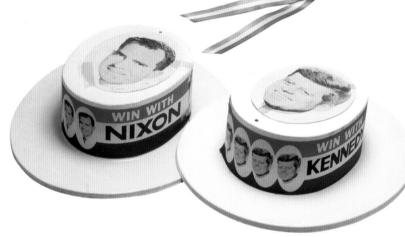

"Win With Nixon" plastic hat with paper pictures of Richard Nixon, 1960, **$15-$25**; and "Win With Kennedy" plastic hat with paper pictures of Kennedy, 1960, **$25-$50**.

Herbert Hoover and Charles Curtis felt cap also touting, on the reverse side, New Jersey candidates "Kean/ Larson/ Hoffman," 1928, 5⅛" x 11" flat, **$50-$75**; and an "I Like IKE" adjustable, rag-quality paper hat, circa 1952-'56, 3½" x 11" flat, **$10-$20**.

"I Like IKE" plastic hats, red, yellow and blue, with embossed faces of Eisenhower and embossed elephants, circa 1952-'56, **$30-$50** each.

TIES

While casual dress in public is much more common today, 40-50 years ago ties were more likely to be used as campaign tools.

Western bolo, yellow string tie with adjustable brass disk framing a black plastic center with image of Lyndon Johnson and the words "Johnson For President;" and an orange string tie with adjustable brass disk framing a white "Johnson For President" plastic center, each circa 1964, 1 5/8" disks, **$15-$25** apiece.

"I Say Adlai" and "Say Adlai" pro-Adlai Stevenson red ties, the latter design including a mirror image of the words, 1952-'56, **$35-$50** each.

A matching pair of campaign ties for the 1948 presidential election showing the Capitol at the top of each tie. "Thomas E. Dewey / 1948" blue tie with his image, **$40-$60**; and "Truman/ 1948" red tie with his image, **$100-$125**.

"Kennedy For President" orange-brown acetate tie with words repeated across the front; clip-on, orange-brown bow tie with "Vote Kennedy For President" and donkey image on bows; and yellow acetate tie with small donkey image at the front top and "Kennedy For President." Ties circa 1960, **$50-$75** each.

T-SHIRTS

One of the most popular types of protest or political campaign clothing is
the T-shirt, particularly in recent years.

Spiro Agnew red, white and
blue cotton T-shirt with caricature design similar to wrist
watch caricature, "Dirty Times,
Inc.," circa 1968-'73, size M,
$20-$30.

"Jimmy Carter For President,"
cotton T-shirt with black
printed image of Carter within
green circular frame, circa
1976, size L 42-44, **$15-$20**.

"Laborers for Clinton-Gore
'96," red, white and blue T-shirt
with gray images of the candidates, "All Sport Proweight,"
size XL 48, **$15-$20**.

"Grits & Fritz/ Our Country's
Hits" red, white and blue cotton T-shirt portraying faces of
Jimmy Carter and Walter Mondale on phonograph record
image, "Pioneer Productions,"
1976, **$15-$20**, size XL 46,
$15-$20.

BELT

"Al Smith Our Next President" leather belt with profile image of Alfred Smith, 1928, 1¼" x 36⅝", **$50-$75**.

BUCKLES

The following three items are probably campaign parade buckles from the
last quarter of the 19th century.

"C & T" buckle for Grover
Cleveland and Allen Thurman,
circa 1888, 2¼" x 3⅜" ,
$75-$100.

"B & L" buckle for James Blaine
and John Logan, circa 1884,
2¼" x 3⅜", **$75-$100**.

"C & S" buckle for Grover
Cleveland and Adlai Stevenson, circa 1892, 2¼" x 3⅜",
$75-$100.

"LBJ" on a cowboy hat at-
tached to a brass (with silver
colored diagonal half) belt
buckle, circa 1964, 1⅜" x 2¾",
$15-$25. Lyndon Johnson's
campaign material usually
stressed a western image.

"Silver" bug buckle for those who favored the free coinage of silver at a 16 to 1 ratio, and a brass "gold" bug buckle for those who favored the gold standard, each circa 1896-1900, 1⅞" diameter, **$35-$50** apiece.

SLIPPERS

Caricature slippers with each designed as a U.S.-flag-covered bed occupied by George H.W. Bush tucked in one and Barbara Bush, wearing a faux-pearl necklace, snug in the other, circa 1988-'92, **$50-$75**.

CANES

Metal, curved handle, wooden cane with "*Jimmy Carter*/ 76" on one side of handle and "*For President*" and image of a donkey head on reverse, "S. B. Outlaw," circa 1976, 35½" long, **$25-$35**.

Wooden cane with metal head of William McKinley, a cast eagle, and the words "Protection/ 1896," circa 1896, 36" long, **$150-$200**. Rough Rider hat was a symbol for Theodore Roosevelt, **$25-$40**.

"Hon. Wm McKinley/ Our Next President" wooden cane (all but 2" cut away) with metal head of William McKinley and words on bust, circa 1896, 5¼" long, **$125-$150**.

Metal, curved handle, wooden cane with "Franklin D. Roosevelt" and small shield image on one side of handle, and "President/ 32" on reverse, circa 1932-'33, 32½" long, rare.

Wooden cane with metal bust of Grover Cleveland and a 2¾" tapered metal tip, circa 1884-'92, 36" long, **$200-$300**.

5

★ ★ ★ ★ ★

PAPER
ITEMS

★ ★ ★ ★ ★ ★ ★ ★

aper items are the most ephemeral campaign pieces, arguably vulnerable to discarding or trashing by humans and the weather. It is all the more necessary to appreciate their historic significance. Because of space limitations, the following are only some of the possible paper categories. 🌿

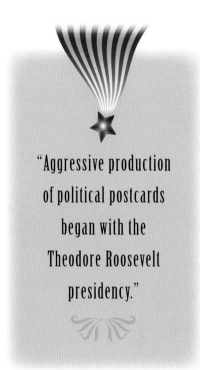

"Aggressive production of political postcards began with the Theodore Roosevelt presidency."

POSTCARDS

Although the picture postcard traces its roots in the United States to the 1890s, aggressive production of political postcards began with the Theodore Roosevelt presidency and had its greatest growth from then until World War I. This was the height of postcard collecting.

After World War I, the color, design and popularity of postcards declined significantly. There were campaign postcards, but most simply depicted the existing president. During the 1970s, reinvigorated collector interest boosted their beauty and historic value. Political cards are usually in the **$5 to $25** range, and all are 3½" x 5½" or slight variations of that size.

Three Theodore Roosevelt cards and one for his 1904 running mate Charles Fairbanks, circa 1900s, **$15-$20** each.

Four Theodore Roosevelt cards, circa 1901-'04, **$15-$25** each. The wedding postcard celebrates the nuptials of Roosevelt's daughter, Alice, and was originally sold with the intention of the customer mailing it to the happy couple. The address side was already imprinted with Alice's address, "Pach Bros.," circa 1904.

Five cartoon Teddy bear postcards refering to Theodore Roosevelt, circa 1906-'08, **$15-$25** each. Note that one card features the bear carrying a big stick and Rough Rider hat.

William Howard Taft/ James Sherman post- cards, 1908, **$15-$25** each.

William Taft postcards, circa 1908-'12, **$10-$20** each.

Four William Taft postcards, circa 1908-'12, **$15-$30** each. Two are real photo cards: an exaggerated postcard using several negatives to display giant crops, and Taft speaking from a train to a large crowd, "W. H. Martin;" and an anti-William Jennings Bryan cartoon postcard meant to depict the images he projected, "M.M. Mabie".

A heavily embossed William Taft campaign card, circa 1908, **$10-$20**; and three Taft cartoon "possum" postcards, circa 1909, **$15-$25** each.

William Bryan/ John Kern postcards, 1908, **$20-$25** each.

William Jennings Bryan picture postcards, circa 1908, **$10-$20** each.

Two pro-William Jennings Bryan postcards, circa 1908, **$35-$50** each. "The Bottom Is Out Of The 'Full Dinner Pail'" puts a twist on the republican slogan. The Bryan caricature card features real textiles and metal buttons.

The "Magic Moving Picture Card" depicts three major candidates for the 1912 presidential election. By moving a tab, the portraits of William Taft, Thomas Woodrow Wilson and Theodore Roosevelt appear sequentially, "A.S. Spiegel," **$25-$50**.

Four Woodrow Wilson cards, circa 1910s, **$10-$20** each. The real photo card of a formally dressed Wilson on horseback holds the highest value.

Four Woodrow Wilson cards, circa 1910s, **$10-$15** each. "Shadow Lawn" was Wilson's "summer White House" in Long Branch, N.J., and although the building is no longer there, the acreage is now part of Monmouth University.

Four women's suffragette cartoon post-cards showing varying levels of support, circa 1910s, **$15-$25** each.

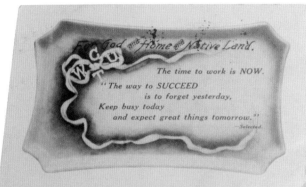

Two anti-alcohol cartoon cards, circa 1900s, **$5-$10** each; and two W.C.T.U. (Women Christian Temperance Union) symbolic poetry cards fighting alcohol addiction, "L.F. Pease," circa 1900s-1910s, **$5-$15** each.

Five Warren Harding postcards, circa 1920-'23, **$15-$20** each. Laddie Boy was Harding's dog.

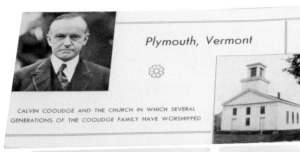

Five Calvin Coolidge postcards, circa 1920s, **$10-$20** each. One of the three photo cards shows Coolidge with Henry Ford, Thomas Edison and others (Firestone?), "Geo. E. Chalmers." Another card is a hand-colored picture of Coolidge, Underwood & Underwood/ The Albertype Co.

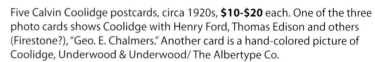

Four cards relating to Franklin Roosevelt, circa 1934-'44, **$10-$15** each. The multicolor patriotic card pictures Roosevelt and images portraying the "Arsenal of Democracy," "Frank T. Perone." The "Three Champions" card (blank on reverse) pictures Roosevelt, former boxing champion Jack Dempsey and New York Gov. Herbert Lehman with the printed signature of Jack Dempsey, circa 1930s, 4¾" x 3".

An anti-Roosevelt caricature card (blank on reverse) with poetic criticism, circa 1936-'40, **$10-$15**; and a Wendell Willkie picture post-card, circa 1940, **$10-$20**.

Three Thomas Dewey campaign cards, **$10-$15** each. Two are for the 1948 presidential election and one card (blank on reverse) urges his election as governor, circa 1940s.

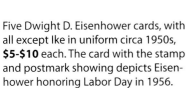

Five Dwight D. Eisenhower cards, with all except Ike in uniform circa 1950s, **$5-$10** each. The card with the stamp and postmark showing depicts Eisenhower honoring Labor Day in 1956.

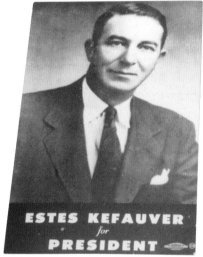

John Kennedy picture card (blank reverse) requesting reader to register democratic, July 1963, **$15-$20**.

"Estes Kefauver For President" card, circa 1954-'56, **$10-$15**.

"Vote John F. Kennedy President" picture card, Nov. 8, 1960, **$10-$15**.

Three Richard Nixon campaign postcards, circa 1960, **$10-$15** each. One is a sample double card, picturing Nixon with reverse reading "I'm for Dick Nixon… ," and a perforated second card connected for bulk ordering the first card, "Kaufmann Printing, Inc."

"He is so highly admired by all his colleagues, not just for his ability, but because of the kind of man he is."
Robert F. Kennedy

"For an Open Convention" questionnaire postcard supporting Eugene McCarthy for president, circa 1968, **$5-$10**; and a postcard picturing George McGovern and wife with supportive comments from the late Robert F. Kennedy, circa 1972, **$5-$10**.

Barry Goldwater color photo card with reverse urging "Goldwater For President," "Lewtan Co.," circa 1964, **$5-$10**.

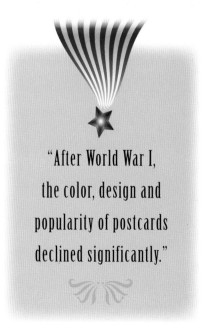

"After World War I, the color, design and popularity of postcards declined significantly."

SHEET MUSIC

During the second half of the 19th and early 20th centuries, the piano was the entertainment center of many American households. The public wanted to learn the lyrics and personally play the music. Sheet music was a popular necessity, and an attractive pictorial cover sheet was likely to increase sales. Today, social historians recognize that old sheet music provides an excellent graphic record of society's attitudes and behavior, including politics and elections.

Confederate sheet music is particularly difficult to obtain. The first two pictures that follow this paragraph show two of about 30 pieces that were bound together with other mid-19th-century sheet music. They dramatize the initial unity and fighting spirit of the Civil War, but as the war dragged on, the quality of the paper was inferior and the song titles reflected longing for the cruel conflict to end.

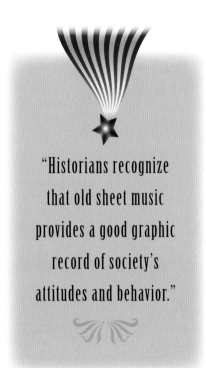

"Historians recognize that old sheet music provides a good graphic record of society's attitudes and behavior."

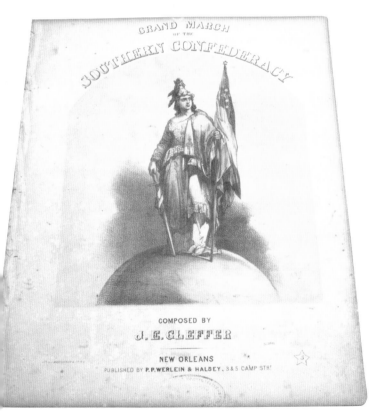

"Grand March of the Confederacy," composed by J. E. Cleffer, published by P.P. Werlein & Halsey, 1861, 9⅞" x 12⅝", rare.

"Jefferson Davis Grand March," composed by C. F. Yeagle, published by Bromberg & Son, 1861, 9⅞" x 12⅝", rare.

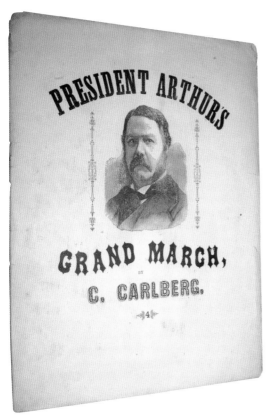

"President Arthur Grand March," composed by C. Carlberg, published by T.F. Loughlin, 1891, 11" x 14", **$35-$50**.

"Cleveland and Hendricks Grand Victory March," composed by J.J. Freeman, published by R. A. Saalfield, 1884, 9¾" x 12", **$75-$125**.

"Blaine and Logan Grand Victory March," composed by J.J. Freeman, published by R. A. Saalfield, 1884, 9¾" x 12", **$75-$125**.

The sheet music introduces three songs for Woodrow Wilson's re-election.
All were published by Leo Feist, 1916, 10½" x 13½", **$20-$30** each:

"Cleveland
Campaign March,"
composed by S.L.
Tyler, published by
F.A. North & Co.,
11" x 14", **$20-$30**.

"Four Years More in the White House," composed by Harold Robe
and Jimmie Morgan.

"Confederate sheet
music is particularly
difficult to obtain."

"The Great American Peace Song/ We Take Our Hats Off to You Mr. Wilson," composed by Blanche Merrill.

"Never Swap Horses When You're Crossing a Stream" composed by Harold Robe and Jesse Winne.

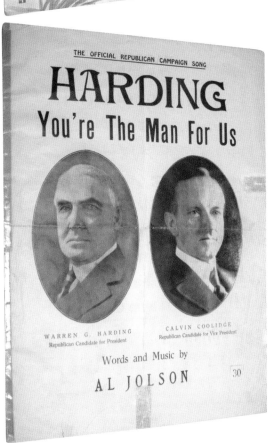

"Harding You're the Man for Us" official republican campaign song, composed by Al Jolson, 1920, 9" x 12", **$20-$35** in excellent condition, **$10-$15** in similar condition.

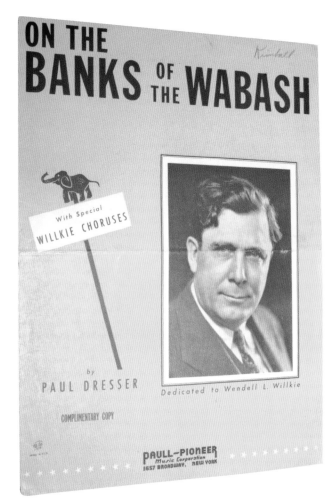

"Return Franklin D. Roosevelt," composed and published by Duke Feher, 1936, 9" x 11⅞", in better condition (no fold marks) **$20-$35**, as is **$10-$15**.

Paul Dresser's "On the Banks of the Wabash" (1897). Because Wendell Willkie was originally from Indiana, the song was converted during 1940 into a political piece with additional pro-Willkie choruses by John W. Bratton, 9"x 12", **$20-$35** in excellent condition, as is **$10-$15**.

National republican song book "We Know Our Business," 23 pages, picturing William McKinley and Theodore Roosevelt on cover, "W.W. McCallip," 1900, 6" x 9⅛", **$15-$25**.

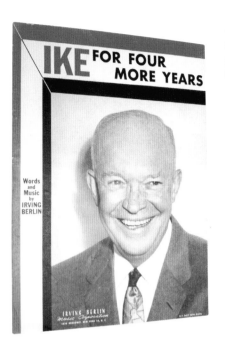

"IKE For Four More Years," "Irving Berlin," 1956, 9" x 12", **$20- $30**.

"A March to Eisenhower" Inauguration song, "Irving Berlin," 1953, 9" x 12", **$20-$30**.

"I Found a Million Dollar Baby" from the Warner Brothers picture "Million Dollar Baby" (1941), Remick Music Corp., circa 1930s, 12" x 9", **$15-$25**. Sheet music picturing Ronald Reagan during his movie career is desirable.

PICTURE POSTERS

Abraham Lincoln-Andrew Johnson-George Washington "Defenders of Our Union" poster with military commanders, circa 1864, 19" x 23", rare.

"General Grant And His Family" poster, "Thomas Kelly," circa 1867, 26¼" x 32¼" in original frame, rare.

President Warren Harding picture poster, Edmonston Studio, 1920, 12⅝" x 18", **$50-$75**.

"For President Alfred E. Smith/ Honest-Able-Fearless" picture poster, circa 1928, 13¾" x 22", **$75-$100**.

"For Vice-President Joe T. Robinson/ Honest-Able-Fearless" poster, circa 1928, 13¾" x 22", **$40-$60**.

Calvin Coolidge-Charles Dawes drawn double poster, "John Doctoroff," circa 1924, 17" x 24", **$75-$100**.

Herbert Hoover-Charles Curtis and New Jersey candidates for senator Hamilton F. Kean and Governor Morgan F. Larson picture poster, 1928, 15⅛" x 23⅛" in frame, **$75-$100**.

Herbert Hoover- Charles Curtis drawn double poster, "John Doctoroff," circa 1928, 18" x 24", **$75-$100**.

Herbert Hoover picture poster reading "Keep Him On The Job," "Bachrach," circa 1932, 16" x 22", **$50-$75**.

Herbert Hoover-Charles Curtis, double picture poster reading "Keep Them On The Job," "Bachrach," circa 1932, 16" x 22", **$75-$100**.

Charles Curtis poster reading "Keep Him On The Job," "Bachrach," circa 1932, 16" x 22", **$40-$60**.

FRANKLIN D. ROOSEVELT

Franklin Roosevelt, drawn image poster, circa 1930s, 12½" x 15⅜", **$50-$75**.

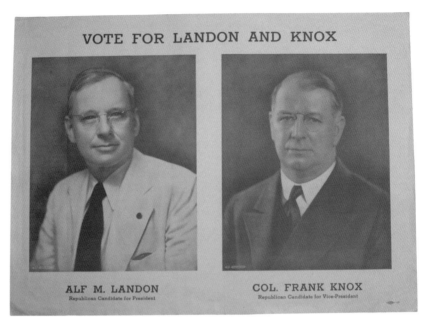

Alf Landon-Col. Frank Knox, double picture poster, circa 1936, 16" x 22", **$75-$100**.

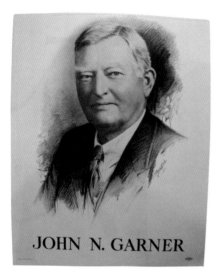

JOHN N. GARNER

John Garner, drawn image poster, circa 1930s, 12½" x 15⅜", **$35-$50**.

"Landon and Knox for the US/ Deeds Not Deficits" red, white and blue poster, 1936, 15" x 31½", **$50-$75**.

Re-elect Dwight D. "Ike" Eisenhower picture poster reading "New Jersey says Yes!," 14" x 22", **$35-$50**.

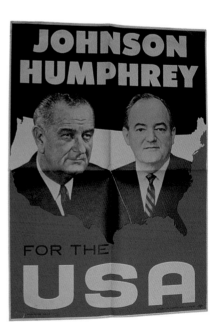

Far right: "Johnson-Humphrey For The USA" poster picturing the candidates, 1964, 20¼" x 28⅜", **$15-$25**.

"Kennedy-Johnson/ two great Democrats" poster, circa 1960, 13¼" x 20⅝", **$75-$125**.

Right: Dwight D. Eisenhower picture poster, convention hall size, circa 1950s, 40½" x 53", rare.

PERSONAL LETTERS

This is a confidential handwritten letter (January 12, 1832) revealing a clever but secret and illegal maneuver of the Andrew Jackson presidential re-election campaign effort. Using the free franking service, a Federal Land Office official informed an Ohio Jackson supporter that the Andrew Jackson Democracy must defeat the Henry Clay Aristocracy. Essentially, he set up a network of supporters and a bimonthly report on "the strength and position of the enemy," 8" x 9¾", rare.

Henry George handwritten and signed letter (note his cabinet photo) explaining that he cannot give up a competitive speaking engagement since "the theater has been engaged and all preparations made," 1890, 5⅜" x 8½", **$100-$200** for letter and photo. George was famous for his "single tax" proposal that government should finance all its projects with money from a single tax on the value of unimproved land since other taxes discouraged productivity and the incentives to earn more money.

Carrie Chapman Catt was president of the National American Woman Suffrage Association. This dictated, typed, signed personal letter revealed that she was planning to take a boat to Asbury Park, N.J., in order to give a talk, 1902, 8⅜" x 10⅞", **$100-$200**.

AUTOGRAPHED OFFICIAL DOCUMENTS

The problem with evaluating and authenticating an autograph is determining whether it is printed, signed by a loyal secretary, a robot pen signature (commonly used by John Kennedy) or simply forged. This demands an expertise beyond most people's ability, but if the item is reasonably priced, seems authentic and would be interesting in any regard, a purchase would be in order. This is especially true when it is a formal document.

Document signed by Peter Cooper, founder of Cooper Union and a greenback candidate for president in 1876, May 1, 1882, 10" x 16", **$200-$300**.

Military commission signed by President Theodore Roosevelt and secretary of war (later president) William Howard Taft, March 29, 1904, **$1,000-$2,000**.

Official document appointing a postmaster signed by Calvin Coolidge, January 10, 1927, 14" x 18", **$150-$250**.

Official Joint Service Achievement Award signed by Secretary of Defense (later vice president) Richard B. Cheney, April 20, 1989, 8" x 10½", **$25-$50**.

THE UNITED STATES OF AMERICA

TO ALL WHO SHALL SEE THESE PRESENTS, GREETING:
THIS IS TO CERTIFY THAT
THE SECRETARY OF DEFENSE
HAS AWARDED

THE JOINT SERVICE ACHIEVEMENT MEDAL

TO

PETTY OFFICER SECOND CLASS DEBORAH L. BURDGE, UNITED STATES NAVY

FOR
MERITORIOUS SERVICE
FOR THE ARMED FORCES OF THE UNITED STATES

GIVEN UNDER MY HAND IN THE CITY OF WASHINGTON
THIS   20TH   DAY OF   APRIL   19 89

OFFICE OF THE SECRETARY OF DEFENSE
COMMAND OR OFFICE

SECRETARY OF DEFENSE

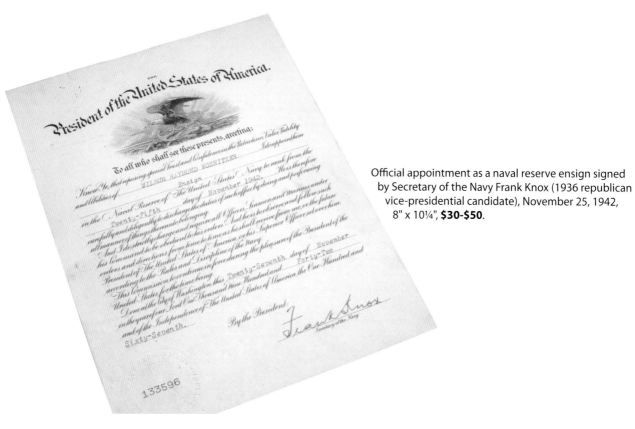

Official appointment as a naval reserve ensign signed by Secretary of the Navy Frank Knox (1936 republican vice-presidential candidate), November 25, 1942, 8" x 10¼", **$30-$50**.

FORM LETTERS AND THANK YOU NOTES

Presidential contenders receive hundreds, if not thousands, of letters every week. Their response or lack of it may encourage loyalty or engender angry displeasure. There are presidential staff members whose major duty is to read those letters and determine what proper printed form letter or card to mail back. The wrong reply might lead to an embarrassing media anecdote.

Soon after he left the presidency in 1953, Harry Truman sent a signed letter thanking a well-wisher. Truman must have received many well-wisher notes, and likely had his response printed. There is no recipient identified, 7¼" x 10", **$30-$50**.

John F. Kennedy signed letter, probably with robot pen, however the letter clearly indicates the importance of maintaining personal and direct communications with the supportive voter, 6⅛" x 8⅛", **$35-$75**.

United States Senate
WASHINGTON, D.C.

January 10, 1961

Miss Marie McMahon
20 Pine Tree Way
Belmar, New Jersey

Dear Miss McMahon:

I want to thank you for the very friendly message you recently sent to me.

I am most heartened by the many expressions of good will which I have received. I am sure that they reflect a broad unity of purpose in our nation. I hope that my record during the next four years will sustain your generous confidence.

With every good wish, I am

Sincerely,

John F. Kennedy

Senator and Mrs. John Fitzgerald Kennedy
gratefully acknowledge your kind wishes
and thoughtfulness
on the birth of their son
John Fitzgerald Kennedy Jr.
November 25, 1960

Mrs. Kennedy is deeply appreciative of
your sympathy and grateful
for your thoughtfulness

The President and Mrs. Kennedy
deeply appreciate your thoughtfulness
and expression of sympathy at this time.

Senator Kennedy and I appreciate
so much the encouragement you have given us
with your thoughts and prayers, and
we want to express our deepest thanks.

Joan Kennedy

The Kennedy family had to endure so many sad occasions, as well as celebrations, that special printed cards were always prepared for mailing to thousands of well-wishers. These, as well as the four cards at top of the following page, are illustrations of the various responses, **$10-$25** each.

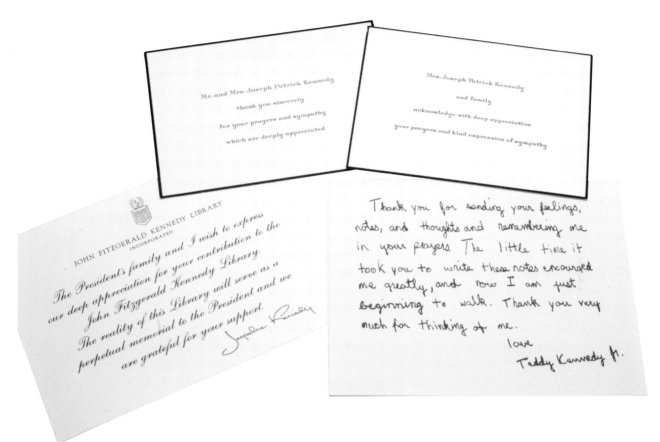

CHRISTMAS CARDS

Two Christmas cards sent by New York Gov. Nelson A. Rockefeller (later, Gerald Ford's vice president) and wife, "Ellsworth Kelly," circa 1967-'69, 5" x 6⅞", **$20-$35** and "View of South Mall," "S. Garrett," circa 1967-'69, 5 1/8" x 6 3/8", **$20-$35**.

Christmas card sent by George and Laura Bush, "Jamie Wyeth/ Hallmark," 2005, 5¼" x 7⅜", **$25-$40**.

Two Christmas cards sent by Jimmy and Rosalynn Carter, "The President's House" (1877) and The White House mid 19th century, "American Greetings," circa 1977-'80, 5½" x 7¼", **$25-$40** each.

CAMPAIGN ENVELOPES

Graphic campaign envelopes are an excellent way to express political views immediately, even before the letter inside is read. Unless noted otherwise, these envelopes are 3⅝" x 6½" or slight variations.

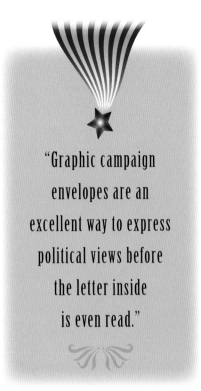

"Graphic campaign envelopes are an excellent way to express political views before the letter inside is even read."

"Votes For Women A Success" envelope with map showing where suffrage has won and urging New Jersey to vote "Yes," 1915, **$35-$50**; "Woodrow Wilson Notification Day" envelope picturing him and a stamp illustrating his "Summer White House" in Long Branch, N.J., 1916, **$20-$30**; and an envelope supporting the "N. R. A. (National Recovery Act)," declared unconstitutional by the Supreme Court in 1935, circa 1933, **$10-$20**.

Anti-Alf Landon card stating that if he had been president in 1933, "there would have been no federal deposit insurance law," circa 1936, **$10-$15**; "Forward with Roosevelt" envelope for the New Deal, circa 1936, **$10-$15**; and a first day cover with Franklin Roosevelt photo attached, 1936, 3⅞" x 7½", **$15-$25**.

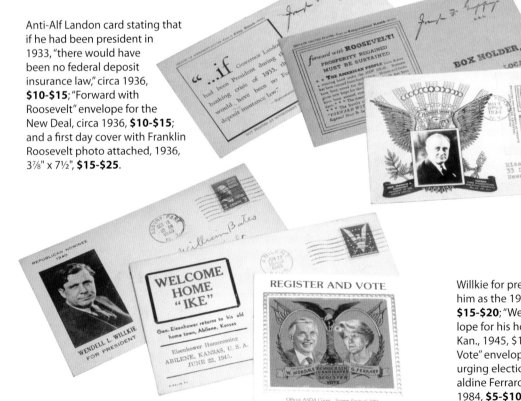

Willkie for president envelop picturing him as the 1940 republican nominee, **$15-$20**; "Welcome Home IKE" envelope for his homecoming to Abilene, Kan., 1945, $10-$20; and a "Register and Vote" envelope with multicolor "silk" urging election of Walter Mondale-Geraldine Ferraro, "Colorano 'silk' Cachet," 1984, **$5-$10**.

PUBLIC MEETING NOTICES AND TICKETS

Announcement for a mass meeting in Montclair, N.J., for Grover Cleveland and Allen Granberry Thurman, 1888, 5½" x 8½", **$15-$25**; and an announcement for a mass meeting in Upper Montclair, N.J., for Cleveland and Adlai Stevenson, October 29, 1892, 5⅜" x 7⅛", rare.

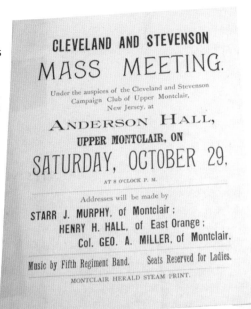

"Congressional Union for Woman Suffrage" typed letter announcing plans for "a nation-wide demonstration" on May 2, 1914, Alice Paul (typed), February 24, 1914, 8½" x 10⅞", **$35-$50**.

"Roosevelt Round-Up Rally" notice for enrollment and registration drive, "Arthur J. Driscoll," 8½" x 10", **$20-$30**.

Communist Party notice for a Union Square demonstration in order to "bury Jim Crow and Hitler with a second front now," circa 1942-'44, 8⅜" x 10⅞", rare.

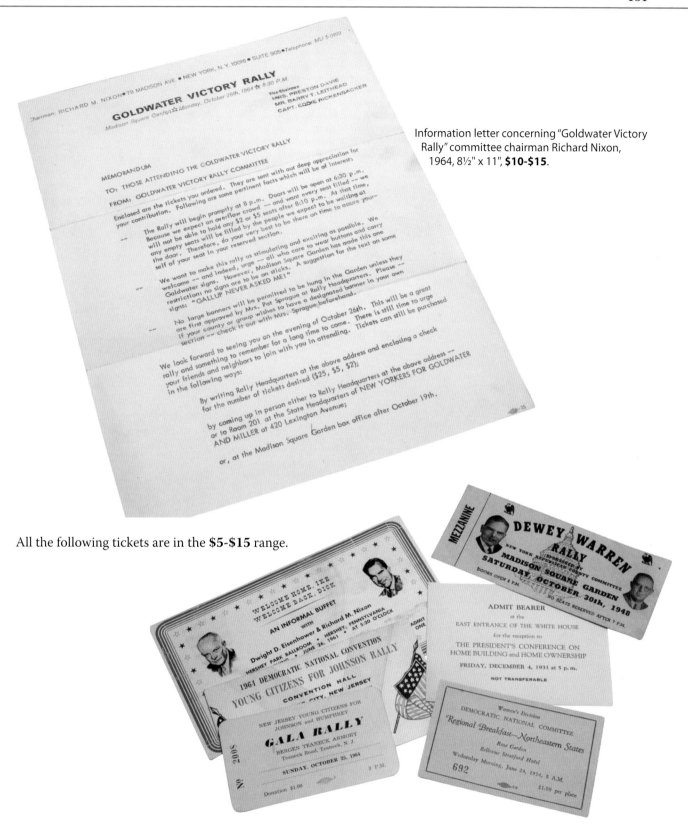

Information letter concerning "Goldwater Victory Rally" committee chairman Richard Nixon, 1964, 8½" x 11", **$10-$15**.

All the following tickets are in the **$5-$15** range.

Ticket for "An Informal Buffet" welcoming Dwight D. Eisenhower and Richard M. Nixon, 1961, 3 7/8" x 6 7/8"; Thomas Dewey-Earl Warren rally ticket, Madison Square Garden, 1948, 2½" x 5¾"; "Young Citizens For Johnson Rally," Atlantic City Convention Hall, 1964, 3" x 5¼"; ticket for president's conference on home building and ownership, 1931, 3¼" x 4½"; rally ticket for Lyndon B. Johnson-Hubert Humphrey, Bergen Teaneck Armory, 1964, 2¼" x 3⅞"; and breakfast ticket from Women Division/ Democratic National Committee, 1936, 2½" x 4".

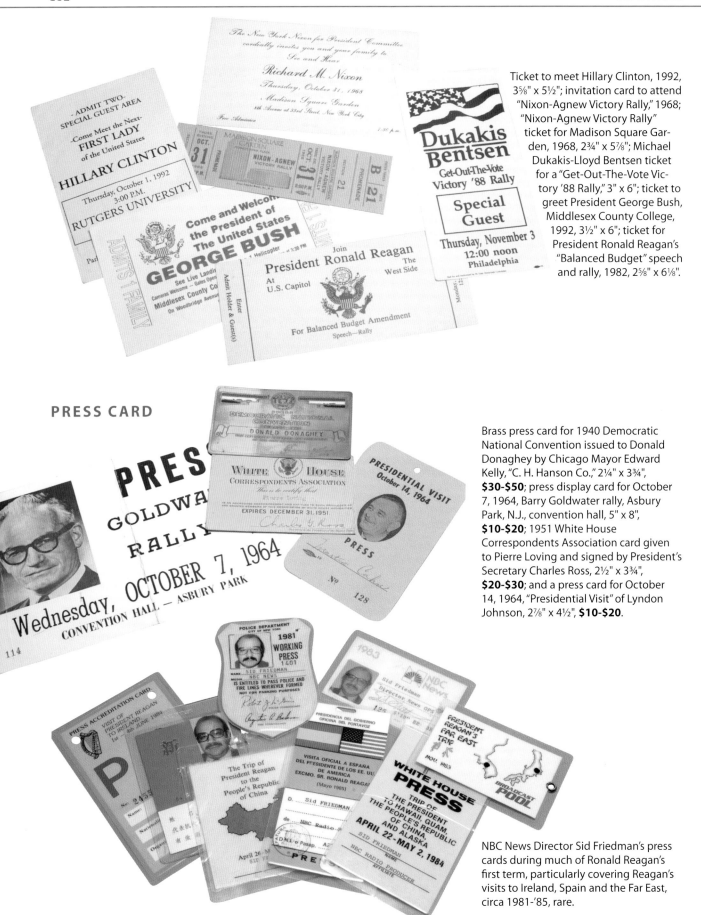

Ticket to meet Hillary Clinton, 1992, 3⅝" x 5½"; invitation card to attend "Nixon-Agnew Victory Rally," 1968; "Nixon-Agnew Victory Rally" ticket for Madison Square Garden, 1968, 2¾" x 5⅞"; Michael Dukakis-Lloyd Bentsen ticket for a "Get-Out-The-Vote Victory '88 Rally," 3" x 6"; ticket to greet President George Bush, Middlesex County College, 1992, 3½" x 6"; ticket for President Ronald Reagan's "Balanced Budget" speech and rally, 1982, 2⅝" x 6⅛".

PRESS CARD

Brass press card for 1940 Democratic National Convention issued to Donald Donaghey by Chicago Mayor Edward Kelly, "C. H. Hanson Co.," 2¼" x 3¾", **$30-$50**; press display card for October 7, 1964, Barry Goldwater rally, Asbury Park, N.J., convention hall, 5" x 8", **$10-$20**; 1951 White House Correspondents Association card given to Pierre Loving and signed by President's Secretary Charles Ross, 2½" x 3¾", **$20-$30**; and a press card for October 14, 1964, "Presidential Visit" of Lyndon Johnson, 2⅞" x 4½", **$10-$20**.

NBC News Director Sid Friedman's press cards during much of Ronald Reagan's first term, particularly covering Reagan's visits to Ireland, Spain and the Far East, circa 1981-'85, rare.

NBC News Director Sid Friedman's press cards during the 1984 Republican National Convention, 3" x 4"; the 1984 political campaign, 2¼" x 4"; and for New York City as a member of the "1984 Working Press," 2⅝" x 4", rare.

DONATION CERTIFICATES

Two Progressive Party donation certificates ($1 and $5) picturing Theodore Roosevelt and Hiram Johnson, 1912, 3¼" x 6¾"; a Home Town Coolidge Club $1 membership certificate picturing Calvin Coolidge, circa 1924, 3" x 5"; and a Thomas Dewey-Earl Warren dollar certificate picturing the candidates, 1948, 3¼" x 7½", **$20-$40** each.

Alfred Smith-Joseph Robinson $5 donation certificate, circa 1928, 7" x 12½", **$35-$50**.

Socialist Party donation certificate, 1936, 8" x 9½", **$35-$50**.

PARTY MEMBERSHIP CARDS

During the 1930s, Socialist Party members carried cards showing (notice stamps) that they paid monthly dues, 5" x 5⅜" open, rare; receipts for the stamps or dues, 3" x 4⅜", **$3-$5** each; and an application form (top) for the Young People's Socialist League, 2¾" x 4¾", **$10-$15**.

TRADE CARDS

During the 19th century, businesses distributed cards advertising their trade or goods. By the 1880s the number of colored cards increased proportionately to their popularity. Sometimes the card designs included the picture of one or both presidential candidates. The best and most thorough early book on trade and other cards is J. R. Burdick's *The American Card Catalog*, Nostalgia Press, Inc., 1967.

"Cherokee Medicine" card showing George McClellan and Abraham Lincoln, 1864, 3" x 5", **$60-$100**.

"Presidential Puzzle" hidden picture card of President Rutherford Hayes, "J. H. Hamburger," 1880, 2¾" x 4⅜", **$25-$40**.

Metamorphic card looks like Samuel Tilton, 1876 Democratic candidate, but when open, there is Ulysses Grant, "Blackwell's Durham Tobacco," circa 1876-'80, 3⅜" x 3⅞" (closed), **$20-$35**.

These are three "Bon-Ton Polish" trade cards picturing Grover Cleveland, Benjamin Butler and James Blaine, 3" x 4⅜" each, circa 1884, **$15-$25** each.

"Practical Politics" card opens to satirize political issues of the day, "The Oliver Chilled Plow," circa 1880s, 6" square, **$10-$20**.

Trade card issued by the Blasius Piano Co. claiming that President Benjamin Harrison endorsed their piano, 1889-'92, 1½" x 2⅞", **$10-$20**.

Two "Stoutenburgh & Co., /Clothier" trade cards, for Benjamin Harrison-Levi Morton and for Grover Cleveland-Allen Thurman, 1888, 3½" x 5", **$15-$25** each.

Cards picturing Grover Cleveland's very popular wife, **$10-$20** each, including multicolor embossed picture card, circa 1886-'88, 1⅞" x 3½"; picture card reading "Use Sulphur Bitters/ Mrs. President Cleveland," circa 1886-'88, 4⅛" x 6⅜"; and Cleveland and his wife, "Nathan Buchwald," circa 1886-'88, 4½" x 5¾".

Trade card with Grover Cleveland on front, and Cleveland and Allen Granberry Thurman on back, "Dambmann Bros. & Co.," circa 1888, 2⅝" x 4½", **$10-$20**; and a James Blaine trade card issued by the Thomas W. Price Co., "wholesale dealers in advertising cards & novelties," 1884, 2½" x 4¾", **$15-$25**.

Three trade cards: two picturing Benjamin Harrison and Levi Morton, as well as Grover Cleveland and Allen Thurman, "Cyrus Lowell" and "Star Clothing Co.," 1888; and one picturing Benjamin Harrison and Whitelaw Reid, as well as Grover Cleveland and Adlai Stevenson, "A.C. Yates & Co.," 1892 , 3⅛" x 4⅝", **$15-$25** each.

James Cox/ Warren Harding advertisement card, "C. S. Garrett & Son Corp.," circa 1920, 5¾" x 9⅛", **$20-$30**; and Theodore Roosevelt and Alton Parker pictured on round advertisement card, "The Delaware and Atlantic Telegraph & Telephone Co.," 1904, 3¾" diameter, rare.

INSERT CARDS

Insert cards are lithographic or photographic cards packed with manufacturers' products. By the mid 1880s, the tobacco industry inserted cards with boxed cigarettes. The cards dealt with virtually unlimited categories, including presidential politics.

Five bubble gum insert cards showing presidential candidates, "T.C.G.," 1972, 2½" x 3½", **$20-$30** for set.

Five insert cards showing "Presidential Possibilities," "Honest Long Cut Tobacco," 1880s, 2½" x 4⅛", **$35-$50** for the set.

Two photograph cards for democratic presidential candidates Winfield Hancock (1880) and Samuel Tilden (1876), "W. Duke, Sons & Co.," circa 1876-'80, 2⅜" x 4", **$30-$50** each.

FAKE OR SATIRICAL MONEY

Fake dollar bills have been produced to ridicule or satirize presidents and presidential contenders. Initially, some may look like real dollars, but instead of picturing George Washington, another politician is shown and ridiculed. Sometimes the dollars support a candidate or issue. These are a few older examples.

"Organize Greenback Clubs" miniature dollar bills with advertisements on reverse, supporting the Greenback Party, circa 1870s-'80s, 1¾" x 3¼", **$15-$25** each.

Anti-New Deal satirical money, Frank C. Hughes, 1936, 2⅝" x 6", **$10-$15**; anti-Lyndon Johnson satirical money, 1966, 2¾" x 6⅜", **$10-$15**; pro-Robert Dole money, "Slick Times," 1996, 2½" x 6¼", **$3-$5;** and anti-Ross Perot satirical money, "Slick Times," 2⅝" x 6⅛", **$3-$5.**

TOBACCO ALBUM

The major tobacco companies produced souvenir albums displaying entire collections of particular political categories. Obtaining the album was usually a reward for sending 75 to 100 coupons that had been accumulated over time from cigarette packages. These albums are usually scarce in excellent condition.

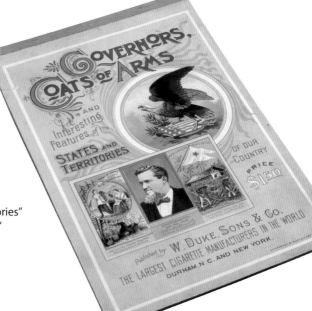

"Governors, Coat of Arms and Interesting Features of the States and Territories" album, published during the Grover Cleveland presidency, circa 1885-'88, " W. Duke, Sons & Co.," 7" x 10", **$50-$100**.

HISTORIC 19ᵀᴴ-CENTURY PRINT

Historic 19th-century presidential campaign lithographic prints have long been collected and many have increased significantly in value. This is just one example.

James K. Polk and George M. Dallas print, in original frame, picturing the candidates and the words "Polk, the Young Hickory/ Dallas and Victory" and "Grand, National Democratic Banner/ Press onward," Nathaniel Currier (before he joined with Ives), circa 1844-45, 12⅞" x 16¼", **$300-$500**.

FRAMED PRINT

During World War II and the resulting metal shortage, it was not unusual for a campaign picture with cardboard backing to be covered by a circular, convex piece of glass and then sealed with paper tape rather than a metal frame.

Gen. Douglas MacArthur patriotic print in a circular, convex frame, "Peter Watson's Studio," circa 1942-'44, 6" diameter, **$20-$30**, presidential hopeful.

Franklin Roosevelt picture in a circular, convex frame, circa 1942-'44, 6½" diameter, **$25-$40**.

CONVENTION TICKETS, SIGN, PROCEEDINGS AND PLATFORMS

Since Andrew Jackson, the major process for nominating presidential candidates has been the national convention. In addition to delegates and other pertinent officials, there are also invited guests occupying gallery seats. Tickets are crucial to maintain control and influence the outcome.

Democratic National Convention, two tickets, 1948, 2¾" x 4⅞", **$10-$15** each.

Democratic National Convention tickets, 1892-1936, **$15-$40** each.

Republican National Convention "pass out check," 1936, 2" x 4", **$10-$15**.

Democratic National Convention, three tickets, 1964, 3¼" x 7⅜", **$5-$10**.

Republican National Convention ticket, 1960, 2⅞" x 5", **$5-$10**.

Republican National Convention, three tickets, 1988, 3" x 5½", **$5-$10** each.

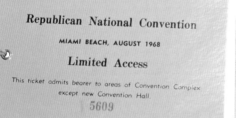

Republican National Convention, three tickets, 2⅞" x 5"; and a "Limited Access" ticket, 3"x 5", 1968, **$5-$10** each.

Democratic National Convention, six tickets from the disruptive convention in Chicago, Ill., 1968, 2⅛" x 3⅜", **$5-$15** each. The tickets are early examples of the type of entry "keys" increasingly used by most major hotels and cruise lines.

"The Democratic Doctrine," democratic platform, keynote speech by Homer Commings and acceptance speech by James Cox, 47 pages, 1920, 6" x 8⅞", **$10-$15;** and "The Republican Doctrine," republican platform, keynote speech by Henry Cabot Lodge and acceptance speech by Warren Harding, 48 pages, 1920, 6" x 8⅞", **$10-$15**.

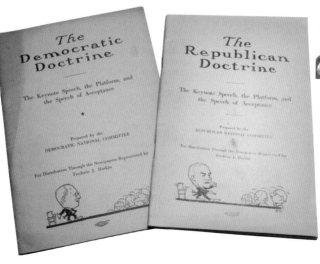

Bill Clinton multicolor image, similar to Elvis stamp, on sign reading "Live from New York Gov. Bill Clinton at Madison Square Garden/ Democratic National Convention/ July 13-16 1992 Delegate," 24" x 36", **$25-$50**.

Below: Official proceedings of the National Democratic Convention held in Cincinnati, Ohio, June 2-6, 1856, 78 pages, 5½" x 8¾", **$20-$30**.

Above left: Republican National Convention Platform, 29 pages, 1964, 5" x 8½", **$5-$10**.

Above center: Democratic National Convention Platform with Franklin Roosevelt quotation and picture on cover, seven-page pamphlet, 1936, 4" x 9", **$10-$20**.

Above right: Communist Election Platform, picturing William Foster and James Ford, 16 pages, 1932, 4¼" x 5⅞", **$20-$30**.

PARTY ELECTION MATERIAL CATALOGS

Two 1964 campaign material catalogs describe material available, as well as names and addresses of suppliers, republican catalog, 35 pages, 8" x 10"; and a democratic catalog, 31 pages, 5¼" x 8¾", **$20-$30** each.

Democratic National Committee Tool Kit for George McGovern and Robert "Sargent" Shriver, including 16 pamphlets, a newspaper, a post-card and a volunteer sign-up sheet, 1972, 10" x 11⅜", **$50-$75**.

PAMPHLETS

Pamphlet showing Woodrow Wilson and James Cox pushing Uncle Sam toward foreign entanglements, circa 1920, 4⅛" x 9¼", **$10-$20**.

Alfred Smith for New York governor, pamphlet, 1918, 4" x 9⅜", **$10-$20**; and "The Women Are With Smith" pamphlet, circa 1918, 3⅞" x 8½", **$10-$20**.

"Independent Voters For Norman Thomas" letter urging a Socialist Party victory, circa 1948, 8½" x 11", **$15-$25**; and a pro-Socialist Party pamphlet urging the election of Norman Thomas and George Nelson, 1936, 7½" x 8½" open, **$20-$30**.

Pamphlet urging Dwight D. Eisenhower nomination at the 1952 Republican National Convention, 1952, 3⅞" x 9", **$10-$20**; and a pro-Eisenhower pamphlet comparing his successes with democratic failures, 1956, 2⅞" x 8⅜", **$10-$20**.

Republican Party pamphlet picturing Thomas Dewey, John Bricker and other republican candidates, 1944, 5⅝" x 8¾", **$10-$20**; and "Democrats For Willkie" pamphlet picturing Uncle Sam and "No Third Term," 1940, 3½" x 8⅛", **$10-$20**.

BOOKLETS

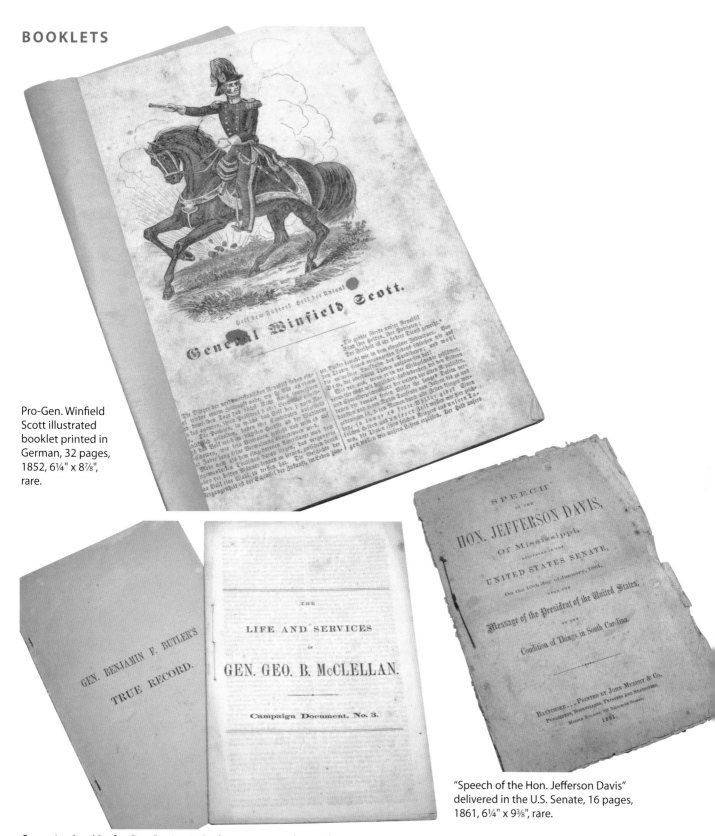

Pro-Gen. Winfield Scott illustrated booklet printed in German, 32 pages, 1852, 6¼" x 8⅞", rare.

"Speech of the Hon. Jefferson Davis" delivered in the U.S. Senate, 16 pages, 1861, 6¼" x 9⅜", rare.

Campaign booklet for Gen. Benjamin Butler, 30 pages, John I. Baker, 1879, 5½" x 8⅝", **$35-$50**; and "Campaign Document No. 3" for Gen. George McClellan, 64 pages, circa 1864, 5⅞" x 8¾", **$35-$50**.

EARLY BALLOTS

Before the adoption of the Australian ballot, each party produced its own ballot with only that party's candidates on it. Each of the official ballots is valued at **$35-$50**.

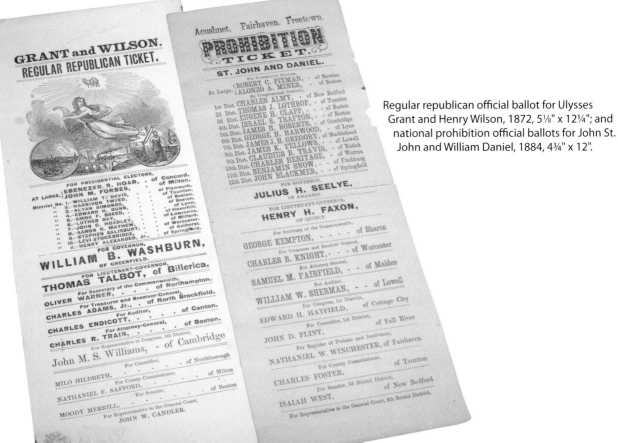

Regular republican official ballot for Ulysses Grant and Henry Wilson, 1872, 5⅛" x 12¼"; and national prohibition official ballots for John St. John and William Daniel, 1884, 4¾" x 12".

AUSTRALIAN BALLOTS

These are some of the earliest examples of Australian ballots being used in the United States. The Australian ballot had all the candidates on one ballot, increasing difficulty in telling how someone voted.

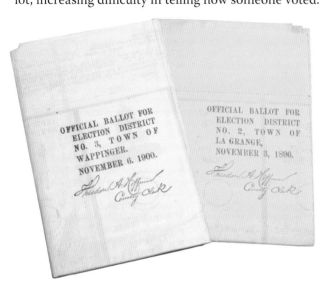

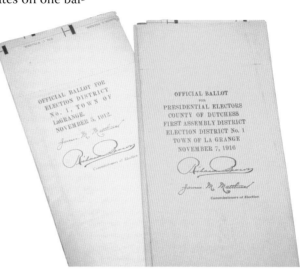

Two official ballots for Town of La Grange, listing all presidential candidates and electors, 18¼" x 20½" open, Nov. 5, 1912, and Nov. 7, 1916, **$20-$30** each.

Official ballot for Town of Wappinger, November 6, 1900, listing all presidential candidates and electors, 15" x 26½" open, **$30-$50**; and official ballot for Town of La Grange, Nov. 3, 1896, listing all presidential candidates and electors, 15" x 26½" open, **$30-$50**.

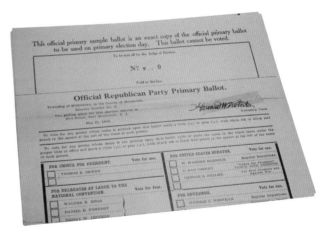

Sample Port Monmouth, N.J., "Official Republican Party Primary Ballot" with only Thomas Dewey's name listed for president, 1940, 9" x 22⅛" open, **$10-$20**.

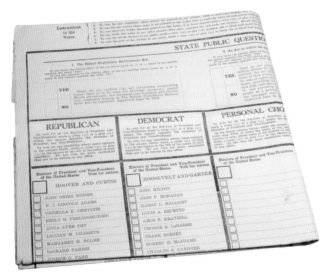

Sample City of Rahway 1932 "Official General Election Ballot" listing all presidential candidates and electors, 19½" x 28¾" open, **$10-$20**.

Sample Port Monmouth, N.J., "Official Democratic Party Primary Ballot" with no name listed for president, 1940, 9" x 22⅛" open, **$10-$20**.

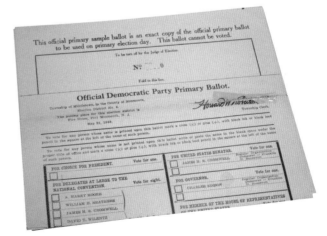

INAUGURATION INVITATIONS AND PROGRAMS

One possible reward for being a political activist, a government leader, a celebrity or a financial supporter is an invitation to an inauguration and/or one of the balls.

Official 1933 inauguration program picturing Franklin Roosevelt and John Garner on the cover, 64 pages, 8½" x 10⅞", **$25-$35**.

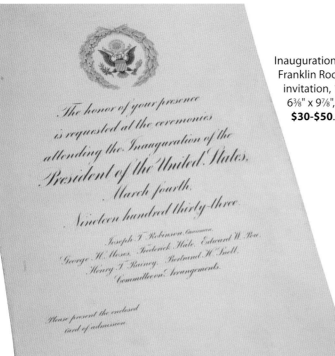

Inauguration for Franklin Roosevelt invitation, 1933, 6⅜" x 9⅞", **$30-$50**.

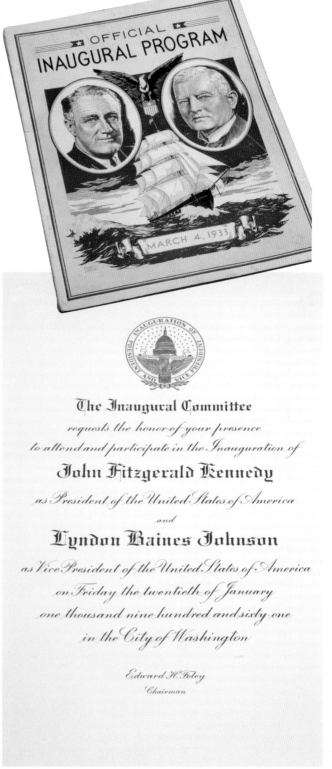

"Inauguration Ceremonies" fully illustrated souvenir booklet published for 1897 inauguration of William McKinley, 48 pages, 7" x 8⅛", **$20-$30**.

Inauguration for John F. Kennedy invitation, 1961, 8⅜" x 11¼", **$25-$40**.

INAUGURATION DAY COVERS

Political collectors seek covers celebrating the January 20th Inauguration Day. The stamp design is not as important as the January 20th date cancellation. The envelope should have a cachet printed on the left side portraying either the president alone or the president and vice president.

There are many cachet designs for each inauguration. Cost depends on the design, the rarity, the condition and the popularity of the president. The typical Inauguration Day cover size is 3⅝" x 6½", unless stated otherwise.

Franklin Roosevelt Inauguration Day cover, March 4, 1933, 3⅞" x 7½", **$10-$20**. The 20th Constitutional Amendment, in 1933, moved inauguration earlier to January 20; Dwight D. Eisenhower cover, "Fleetwood," 1957, **$5-$10**; and John F. Kennedy cover, "Fleetwood," 1960, **$5-$10**.

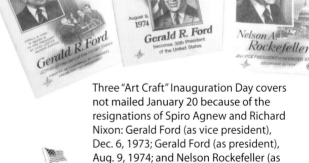

Two "Art Craft" covers for Richard Nixon, 1969, and Lyndon Johnson, 1965, **$3-$5** each.

Three "Art Craft" Inauguration Day covers not mailed January 20 because of the resignations of Spiro Agnew and Richard Nixon: Gerald Ford (as vice president), Dec. 6, 1973; Gerald Ford (as president), Aug. 9, 1974; and Nelson Rockefeller (as vice president), Dec. 19, 1974, **$5-$10** each.

Each of these four covers, produced by "Art Craft," is valued at **$3-$5**: Jimmy Carter, 1977; Ronald Reagan, 1985; George Bush, 1981; and Bill Clinton, 1993.

6

KITCHENWARE

AND

GROCERY ITEMS

CERAMIC PLATES

Throughout our country's history, ceramic pieces have long been designed to appeal to the political and patriotic fervor of Americans. British potters created china for the American export market and those pieces from the first 40 to 50 years of our country's existence are highly prized, rather rare and usually quite expensive.

Most of the pieces honored George Washington and, to a lesser degree, other early presidents. Starting mainly with the 1840 election of William Henry Harrison, and more frequently during the 1880s, American pottery firms produced an increasing number of campaign plates and other ceramic pieces.

If one walked around the flea markets during the 1960 to 1980 period, most dealers were not interested in campaign plates. This still appears to be true in regard to current and recent election ceramics.

Most plates display all the presidents up until the date the plate was produced or are Washington souvenir shop plates of the existing president. Because of space limitations, with certain exceptions, these are not illustrated. Nevertheless, many political plates have become increasingly difficult to obtain. They are important examples of our political history.

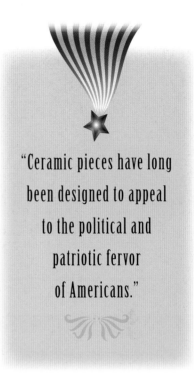

"Ceramic pieces have long been designed to appeal to the political and patriotic fervor of Americans."

James Blaine plate, 8¼" diameter, circa 1884, **$75-$100**.

Grover Cleveland plate, 9⅛" diameter, "Opaque Porcelain," circa 1884, **$100-$150**.

Thomas Hendricks plate, 9¼" diameter, "Opaque Porcelain," circa 1884, **$100-$150**.

William McKinley-Garret Hobart plate with gold floral design around the scalloped border, 8½" diameter, "Jesse Dean/China Decorator," circa 1896, **$75-$100**.

Thomas Hendricks plate, 8" diameter, "Imperial Warranted China," circa 1884, **$75-$100**.

William McKinley-Garret Hobart plate, 9" diameter, "John Maddock & Sons Royal Vitreous," circa 1896, **$75-$100**.

William McKinley plate, 7¼" diameter, "A.K./France/ Jesse Dean/ China Decorator," circa 1896, **$50-$75**.

Garret Hobart plate, 7⅜" diameter, "A.K./ France/ Jesse Dean/ China Decorator," circa 1896, **$40**.

Adm. George Dewey, 1900 presidential hopeful, plate, 9" diameter, "Baltimore Ceramic Co.," circa 1899-1900, **$50-$75**.

Theodore Roosevelt plate, 9½" diameter, "O.P. Co. China," circa 1916, **$30-$60**.

"Our Choice 1908," William Bryan plate, 8½" diameter, "Carrollton China," **$75-$100**.

"Our Choice 1908," William Taft plate, 7½" diameter, "Carrollton China," **$75-$100**.

"An Invincible Combination/ Smiling Bill/ Sunny Jim," platter with images of William Taft and James Sherman, 9" x 6⅜", "Warwick China," circa 1908, **$75-$100**.

Similar to plate at left, but plate with images of William Taft and James Sherman, 8¼" diameter, "Dresden China," circa 1908, **$75-$100**.

William Taft-James Sherman multicolor plate with roses, flags and an eagle, 7⅜" diameter, "The Goodwin Pottery Co.," circa 1908-'12, **$75-$100**.

Woodrow Wilson plate, 5⅞" diameter, "Semi Porcelain/ HP Co.," circa 1912-'18, **$50-$75**.

Woodrow Wilson Camp Dix plate, 6" diameter, "Semi Porcelain/ HP Co.," circa 1916-'18, **$50-$75**.

Charles Evan Hughes plate, 10¼" diameter, "Bristol," circa 1916, rare.

Franklin Roosevelt picture plate with gold-decorated blue border, 9⅞" diameter, CAPSCO, 1940s, **$35-$50**.

Franklin Roosevelt picture plate with Allied Nations flags around rim, 10⅝" diameter, "The Salem China Co.," circa 1943-'45, **$50-$75**.

Gen. Douglas MacArthur, 1952 presidential hopeful, plate with Allied Nations flags around rim, 10⅞" diameter, "The Salem China Co.," circa 1943-'45, **$25-$40**.

Gen. Douglas MacArthur plate, 10½" diameter, "Vernon Kilns," circa 1943-'44, **$25-$40**.

1953 inauguration plate, 10⅝" diameter, "Decorated by Delano Studio," **$25-$40**.

"Republican Centennial/ 1854 Freedoms Fight From ABE to IKE … 1954," 9¼" diameter, "Kettlesprings Kilns … RDI," **$25-$40**.

"1854/ Republican Centennial / 1954," souvenir plate distributed by the Camden County Republican Assoc. at an Oct. 13, 1954, dinner, **$25-$40**.

John Kennedy and Pope John XXIII plate, 10" diameter, Italy, circa 1961-'63, **$25-$35**.

President and Mrs. John Kennedy plate, 10⅞" diameter, "Capsco, 1961," **$35-$50**.

President and Mrs. John Kennedy plate, 6⅛" diameter, circa 1961-'62, **$25-$35**.

Florida welcomes the Republican National Convention to Miami Beach, 9¾" diameter, "The Walker China Co.," 1968, **$20-$30**.

Richard Nixon profile porcelain plate, Wedgwood, circa 1969, 4⅜" diameter, **$30-$50**.

President and Mrs. Gerald Ford plate, 9¼" diameter, circa 1974-'76, **$20-$30**.

Jimmy Carter plate, with 1977 inauguration on reverse, 10¼" diameter, **$20-$30**.

Jimmy Carter and flag plate, 10¾" diameter, "Heritage Fine China," **$20-$30**.

CERAMIC MUGS

Ceramic mug with caricature of a cigar-smoking Al Smith, 4" high, 3⅜" diameter base, "Stangl," circa 1920s, **$75-$100**.

Franklin Roosevelt white figural mug, 4⅝" high, 3 x 3½" diameter, Patriotic Products Assoc., circa 1930s, **$50-$75**.

Gen. Douglas MacArthur ceramic mug with image in uniform and with sword as handle, 5¼" high, 3⅝" x 3⅛" base, "Royal Winton," circa 1944-'52, **$50-$75**.

John Kennedy mug, 3⅛" high, 2½" diameter base, circa 1960-'63, **$20-$25**.

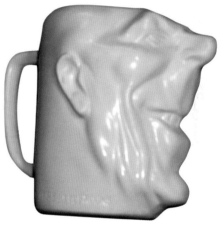

"Bobby [Kennedy] For President," mug, 3⅞" high, 2¾" diameter, "Mann Made Mugs/ exclusive," **$25-$40**.

Satirical anti-Richard Nixon mug with worthless "Federal Reserve Note," 3½" high, 3" diameter, "HH," circa 1972, **$10-$20**.

Ronald Reagan caricature face mug, 3⅞" high, 2⅛" x 2½" base, J.M. Brooks, circa 1985, **$20-$30**.

Jimmy Carter caricature face mug, 4" high, 3⅝" diameter, circa 1976-'80, **$15-$25**.

Jimmy Carter smiling, toothy peanut mug, 4⅜" high, 2¼" diameter, "Trimple Corp.," circa 1976-'80, **$15-$25**.

Anti-Bill Clinton mug, 3¾" high, 3⅛" diameter, First Amendment Products, circa 1993, **$5-$10** each.

GLASS PLATES, CUPS AND PITCHERS

Glass platter with images of Benjamin Harrison and Levi Morton, as well as leaf images bordering rim, 4¾" x 5¾", circa 1888, **$100-$150**.

Whig political glass plate displaying Henry Clay's reputed image, 5⅝" diameter, a few chips along the border edge, circa1840s, **$50-$100**.

Whig political glass plate displaying the image of a log cabin and barrel of hard cider, William Henry Harrison's campaign symbol, 3¼" diameter, some small chips along border edge, circa 1840, **$75-$125**.

Glass plate with embossed image of Benjamin Harrison and with "Give Us This Day Our Daily Bread" along rim, 4¾" diameter, circa 1888-'92, **$100-$150**.

Glass plate with John Logan's embossed image, 7⅜" diameter, circa 1880s, **$75-$100**. Logan was leader of the Union veterans Grand Army of the Republic (GAR) and the republican vice-presidential candidate in 1884.

"The Patriot and Soldier/ Gen. Ulysses S. Grant," glass platter, 9½" x 9½", circa 1860s-'70s, may be a memorial from 1885, **$50-$75**.

Glass with James Garfield's embossed image in the flat bottom, 3⅝" high, 2½" diameter, circa 1880-'81, **$50-$75**.

Glass plate with embossed image of James Garfield and stars around rim, 6" diameter, circa 1880-'81, **$50-$75**.

Decorated glass cup with William McKinley's embossed image and reading "Protection and Prosperity," 3½" high, 2⅝" diameter, hairline cracks at top, circa 1896, **$25-$35**.

Glass with Ulysses Grant's image and reading "Fraternity/ Loyalty/ Charity," 3¾" high, 2⅜" diameter, circa 1860s, **$60-$75**.

Franklin Roosevelt glass, 4¾" high, 2⅛" diameter, circa 1932-'44, **$25-$35**.

Glass with image of Adm. George Dewey, "The Nelson of America," 3¾" high, 2¼" diameter, circa 1899-1900, **$30-$40**.

Adm. George Dewey glass pitcher featuring his flagship *Olympia*, 9¼" high, 4" diameter base, circa 1899-1900, **$100-$150**.

SALT AND PEPPER SHAKERS

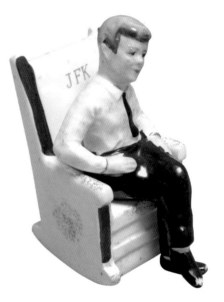

Ceramic peanut salt and pepper shakers with Jimmy Carter's smiling, toothy grins, 3⅜" high, circa 1976-'80, **$25-$35**.

President and Mrs. Richard Nixon, salt and pepper shakers, circa 1969-'73, 2⅞" high, 2⅛" diameter, **$20-$25**.

China two-piece salt and pepper shaker set depicting John Kennedy sitting on a rocking chair, "Arrow," circa 1962, 2" x 3", 4" high, **$50-$75**. Sitting on a rocking chair apparently eased the pain in Kennedy's bad back. The rocking chair emerged as a campaign symbol and probably would have been used more during his intended re-election effort. See examples in the jewelry chapter.

Two President and Mrs. John Kennedy salt and pepper shaker sets, circa 1961-'63 , **$25-$35** each.

TILES

Grover Cleveland intaglio tile portrait, "C. Pardee Works," circa 1884-'96, 6" square, ½" high, **$100-$125**.

William McKinley intaglio tile portrait, "American Encaustic Tiling Co.," circa 1896, 2⅞" square, ¼" high, **$75-$100**.

"1956 IKE + Dick" tile with image of well-dressed elephant rollerskating, 4⅜" square, **$5-$15**.

Woodrow Wilson blue six-sided tile with white, embossed image, "The MosaicTile Co.," circa 1916, 1¾" each side, ½" high, **$75-$100**.

Tile picturing Jimmy Carter and Virginia candidates Chuck Robb, Henry Howell and Ed Lane, 1977, 6" square, **$10-$20**.

Calvin Coolidge intaglio tile profile portrait, circa 1923-'28, 2⅞" x 4⅜", some minor edge chips, ⅜" high, **$75-$100**.

"Mag. Gen. W. S. Hancock," wood collar box with cover displaying Hancock's image composed of pressed gum shellac and woody fibers similar to daguerreotype Union cases "American Miniature Case Art, Floyd and Marion Rinehart, A. S. Barnes and Company, London, p. 31), circa 1880, 3⅜" high, **$250-$350**.

"Gen. James A. Garfield," composition material cover displaying Garfield's image in a form similar to collar box covers, but it was produced with an advertisement on the reverse for S. Peck & Co., "Manufacturer of goods from plastic material," circa 1880, slightly less than 4" square, **$250-$350**.

President and Mrs. John Kennedy ceramic hot plate picturing the couple, circa 1961-'62, 3½" diameter, **$20-$25**.

CERAMIC BUSTS

Porcelain medal with image of Rutherford B. Hayes, 1¾" diameter, "Union Porcelain Works," circa 1876-'80, rare.

Ceramic bust of Vice President William Wheeler, 6½" high, 3⅝" x 3¼", "Brewer," circa 1870s, rare.

William McKinley Parian (Parian marble) bust, circa 1896-1900, 4¾" high, 1¼" diameter, circa 1896-1900, **$40-$60**.

James Garfield Parian bust, circa 1880-'81, 5¼" high, 1⅞" diameter, **$40-$60**.

OTHER CERAMIC PIECES

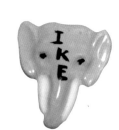

Oval porcelain piece with embossed image of William Taft, 1⅜" x 2", "P. Korzilius," circa 1908, **$75-$100**.

Herbert Hoover white ceramic figural pitcher (left), 7" high, 5½" x 5¼", "Patriotic Products Association," **$100-$150**; and a miniature ceramic Hoover pitcher, 2" high, 1¼" square, circa 1928-'32, **$20-$30**.

"We Like IKE" ceramic nodding/bobbling head (pin holder?), 4" high, circa **$75-$100**.

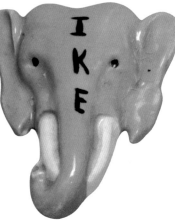

Two sizes of "IKE" ceramic, flat elephant heads, circa 1952-'56, 1⅞" x 2⅜" and ⅞" x 1", **$5-$15** each.

Porcelain stud with image of William McKinley, ⅝" diameter, "O'HARA Co.," circa 1896-1900, **$75-$100**.

"I Like IKE" ceramic pin with fingers forming the "V" for victory sign, circa 1952-'56, 1⅜" x 1⅜", **$15-$25**.

PAPER CUPS

Paper campaign cup picturing Richard Nixon and George McGovern, "Maryland Cup Corp.," 1972, 3⅛" high, 2" diameter, **$5-$10**.

"I'm Voting for Gore" and "I'm Voting For Bush" paper cups issued in 2000 by 7-Eleven Stores, 2⅜" diameter, 5⅞" high, **$2-$5** each.

Pro-George W. Bush and pro-John Kerry "7-Election 2004" paper cups issued by 7-Eleven Stores, 2½" diameter, 6" high, **$2-$5** each.

BEER AND SODA CANS

BOTTLES

"I Like IKE" soda can with image of an elephant holding a pro-Dwight D. Eisenhower flag, circa 1952-'56, 2⅝" diameter, 4¾" high, **$25-$35**.

"The Right Drink For The Conservative Taste" soda can for Barry Goldwater, "Gold-water Distributing Co.," circa 1964, 2⅝" diameter, 4¾" high, **$20-$30**.

"Billy Beer" refers to Jimmy Carter's brother, Billy Carter, who received some attention during Jimmy's campaign, "The West End Brewing Co.," circa 1977-'80, 2½" diameter, 4¾" high, **$5-$10**.

Two campaign bottles: green Hubert Humphrey-Edmund Muskie bottle, and an amber Richard Nixon-Spiro Agnew piece, "Wheaton Glass Co.," circa 1968, 7" high, 2½" x 6" at base, **$15-$25** each.

Liquor bottle celebrates the 1953 Inauguration of Dwight D. Eisenhower and Richard Nixon, 11½" high, 3" diameter, **$35-$50**.

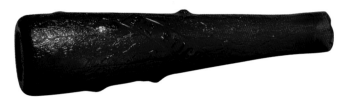

"Big stick" (an apparent reference to Theodore Roosevelt's expression "walk softly but carry a big stick") glass bottle in the shape and style of a club, and with "Patented March 19, 1907" on the bottom, 6⅞" high, 1½" diameter, **$35-$50**.

CORK BOTTLE STOPPERS AND SODA BOTTLE COVER

During the early1950s, a number of cork bottle stoppers were produced that showed political leaders and presidential hopefuls.

CANDY OR SOAP MOLDS

Dwight Eisenhower cork bottle stopper, circa 1950-'53, 2½" high, **$50-$75**.

Gen. Douglas MacArthur cork bottle stopper, circa 1950-'53, 3⅜" high, **$40-$60**.

Two-part metal mold designed to produce three Rough Rider uniformed Theodore Roosevelt candies or soaps, circa 1899-1904, 5⅞" x 1¾", 2⅝" high, rare.

Barry Goldwater-Bill Miller plastic soda bottle cover, circa 1964, 3¾" long, **$5-$10**.

NAPKIN

Two-part metal mold designed to produce three candies or soaps in the shapes of ships (Adm. Dewey's *Olympia* ship?), circa 1899-1904, 9⅛" x 1¾", 1½" high, **$75-$125**.

Pro-Alf Landon paper napkin with his image on a large sunflower and anti-Franklin Delano Roosevelt and Jim Farley lyric along the border, "ELB," circa 1936, 13½" square, **$20-$30**.

CIGAR BOXES AND LABELS

During the 1880s, cigar brands often visually honored prominent figures with lithographed portrait labels. Sometimes only candidate names were printed on the cigar boxes.

Benjamin Harrison and Whitelaw Reid wooden cigar box, "Paramount Cigar Factory," circa 1892, 4¾" x 3", 1⅞" high, **$50-$75**.

"Cleveland & Thurman," multicolor sample label, "Johns & Co.," circa 1888, 8" x 6", **$50-$75**.

"Square Deal" (Theodore Roosevelt slogan) cigar box with multicolor picture and words "Justly Popular," 5⅜" x 8⅝", 2½" high, **$35-$60**.

Franklin Roosevelt cigar box with picture on inside cover, circa 1930s, 5¾" x 9⅜", 2½" high, **$35-$60.**

CIGARS AND CIGAR BANDS

Cigar bands wrapped around cigars advertise the cigar companies, but they may also reveal the political support of those smoking the cigar or giving it away.

Two multicolored, embossed cigar bands: William Bryan and William Taft, circa 1908, 6" x 2½" (Taft band is folded), **$20-$25** each.

Two Souvenir National Convention cigar bands: "1948 Phila., PA." (4¾" x 2⅝") and "1952 Chicago, ILL." (5½" x 2⅝"), **$5-$10** each.

Two campaign cigars: John F. Kennedy/ Lyndon B. Johnson and Richard Nixon/ Henry Cabot Lodge, 1960, 10" long, **$40-$60** each.

Two anti-prohibition labels.

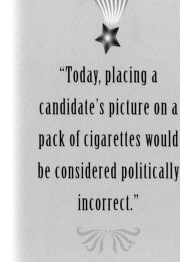

CIGARETTE PACKS AND CIGARETTE PAPER

Today, placing a candidate's picture on a pack of cigarettes would be considered politically incorrect. At one time, however, it was a great way to reward a potential voter and encourage a public display of one's views every time a cigarette was removed from a pack.

Two cigarette packs: "Bush for President" and "Dukakis for President," "G.L. Georgopulo & Co.," circa 1988, 2⅛" x ¾", 3⅜" high, **$15-$25** each.

"I Like IKE" cigarette pack, "Tobacco Blending Corp.," **$25-$50**.

> "Today, placing a candidate's picture on a pack of cigarettes would be considered politically incorrect."

"Joint Staff," anti-Spiro Agnew caricature on cardboard holder and rolling paper, circa 1969-'73, 3⅛" x 1⅞", **$20-$30**.

Richard Nixon cigarette box reading "I want to make it perfectly clear (an expression frequently used by Nixon) I'm for Nixon," "G.L. Georgopulo & Co.," circa 1972, 3⅝" x 2⅞", 2¾" high, **$15-$25**.

BUBBLE GUM CIGARS

From circa-1960 to present, bubble gum political cigars have become increasingly more popular election promoters than real cigars. Unless otherwise noted, the following were produced by "Swell/Philadelphia Chewing Gum Corp."

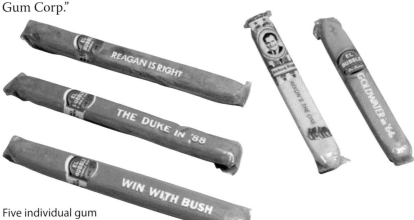

Five individual gum cigars: "Reagan Is Right," circa 1984, 5¾" long, **$5**; "The Duke In '88," circa 1988, 5¾" long, **$5**; "Win With Bush," circa 1988, 5¾" long, $5; "Nixon's The One," "The Donruss Co.," circa 1968, 4⅜" long, **$10-$20**; and "Goldwater in '64," circa 1964, 4¼" long, **$10-$20**.

Two full cases of George W. Bush and Al Gore bubble gum cigars circa 2000, 5⅜" x 6¼", 1½" high, **$20-$30** each.

Full case of Walter (Fritz) Mondale gum cigars, circa 1984, 5⅜" x 6⅜", 1½" high, **$35-$50**.

PIPES

During the 19th century, it was not uncommon for famous political leaders to be subjects of pipe designs.

Display case picturing George H. W. Bush, circa 1988, 5⅜" x 6¼", 1½" high, **$10-$15**.

William McKinley clay pipe, without stem, in Napoleon-style hat and coat, 3⅛" high, circa 1896-1900, **$100-$150**.

Spiro Agnew ceramic pipe with caricatured face as bowl and with handle composed of red, white and blue wooden balls, circa 1969-'73, 4¼" long, **$30-$50**.

METAL MATCHBOXES AND HOLDERS

Before safety matches became widely available in the early 20ᵗʰ century, matches were kept in metal containers, with non-safety matches too dangerous to leave uncontained.

"Teddy B" metal matchbox with embossed image of a bear holding a club and a Rough Rider hat. The reverse touts the "Congress Hotel," circa 1904-'08, ⅜" x 1½", 2¾" high, **$100-$125**.

"Hero of Manila/ May 88," Adm. George Dewey brass match holder, circa 1898-1900, ½" x 1⅛", 2¾" high, **$25-$35**.

Leather-covered metal matchbox with silver-plated copper bust of Adm. George Dewey attached to front and "Fred Muth Harmonie Hall" advertisement on reverse, circa 1899-1900, ⅜" x 1½", 2¾" high, **$35-$50**.

Adm. Dewey metal bust matchbox holder, circa 1899-1900, 1½" x 2⅜", 3½" high, **$35-$50**.

MATCHBOOKS

Cardboard was enough to enclose safety matches and still provide security. Printed promotional advertisements encouraged giving the matches away free, and matchbooks made great political campaign media. Every time a smoker used a match, he saw the candidate's picture and/or appeal.

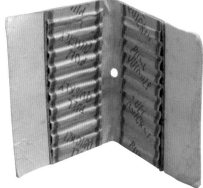

"Repeal," an anti-prohibition matchbook, circa pre-1933, **$5-$10**.

Franklin Roosevelt matchbook welcoming the Chicago Democratic National Convention, circa 1940, **$15-$20**.

"Kennedy for President," red, white and blue matchbook picturing John F. Kennedy, circa 1960, **$15-$20**.

Wendell Willkie for president matchbook that automatically lit matches when they were pulled from their individual sleeves, "American Pullmatch Div.," circa 1940, 2" x 2¼", **$15-$20**.

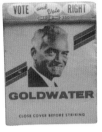

Four 1964 Barry Goldwater for president matchbooks, 1964, **$5-$10** each; and one matchbook welcoming delegates to the 1964 Democratic Women's Campaign Conference, **$5-$10** each.

Three pro-Dwight D. Eisenhower matchbooks, **$5-15** each: "Keep IKE in the White House" matchbook, circa 1956; a "Stick with IKE" matchbook capable of sticking to a cigarette pack and, on the inside, promoting a Madison Square Garden "Salute to Eisenhower Rally," 1956; and a "Newsday We Like IKE" publication endorsement, circa 1952.

Thomas Dewey-John Bricker matchbook listing republican candidates in the national and New Jersey county election, circa 1944, 3" x 2" closed, **$10-$20**.

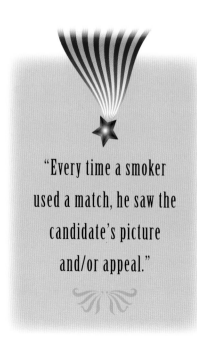

"Every time a smoker used a match, he saw the candidate's picture and/or appeal."

Wendell Willkie matchbook displaying, when opened, a die-cut Willkie picture and matchstick figures of five Americans standing above the words "We the people want Willkie," 1940, **$25-$35**.

Two "Vote Democratic" matchbooks, one picturing Lyndon Johnson and Hubert Humphrey, the other only picturing Johnson, circa 1964, **$5-$10** each.

CIGARETTE LIGHTERS

Cigarette lighter with picture of Lyndon Johnson on one side and Hubert Humphrey on the other side, "Life-Liter Ritepaint," circa 1964-'68, 2⅛" high, **$25-$35**.

Butane gas lighter with caricature of George H. W. Bush dressed as weapon-carrying "soldier of fortune," "King," circa 1988-'92, 3¼" high, **$10-$20**.

Brass cigarette lighter with "President Roosevelt" imprinted on one side, 2⅜" high, **$25-$35**.

Cigarette lighter with red, white and blue stripes and elephant image, "Amico Import," circa 1964, 2¼" high, **$10-$15**.

ASHTRAYS

"Adlai Stevenson" red-brown-enamel metal ashtray with signed name in gold, circa 1952-'56, 3½" square, **$25-$35**.

"Dwight Eisenhower" blue-enamel metal ashtray with signed name in gold, circa 1952-'56, 3½" square, **$25-$35**.

"Stevenson/ Kefauver" metal ashtray with two metal donkeys, "A Hamilton Product," circa 1956, 4½" diameter, **$25-$40**.

"Dick Nixon" brown glass ashtray with gold lettering reading "Thanks To A Key Leader," apparently given as a gift, 1960, 3⅝" square, **$25-$35**.

Same as at left, but also "Bill Miller/ Chairman/ National Republican Congressional Committee." Miller was the 1964 republican candidate for vice president, **$25-$35**.

President and Mrs. John Kennedy multicolor ceramic ashtray adorned with the couple's picture, circa 1961-'62, 4¾" x 6¾", **$20-$30**.

TRAYS

Metal tray with cardboard multicolored picture of Barry Goldwater, circa 1964, 8⅜" diameter, **$15-$20**.

"Keep Roosevelt in the White House," rectangular, multicolor metal tray of the White House with inset picture of Franklin Roosevelt, circa 1936-'40, 10½" x 13¼", 1¼" high, **$50-$60**.

Metal change tray picturing presidential hopeful Adm. George Dewey, circa 1899-1900, 5¾" diameter, ¼" high, **$25-$50**.

"The White House," same as above but sold after the election since it has a different decal lettering on the bottom rim, **$35-$50**.

William Taft/ James Sherman multicolored display tray picturing them and other republican contenders since 1856, 1908, 10" diameter, **$100-$150**.

Theodore Roosevelt-Charles Fairbanks aluminum tray sporting their pictures and that of the White House, "Strong in Conquest," "Aluminum Mfg. Co.," circa 1904-'08, 9¼" x 3⅞", **$50-$75**.

FIRST AID KIT

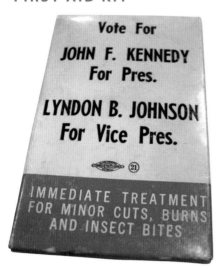

Jon F. Kennedy-Lyndon B. Johnson first aid kit, including three bandages and two antiseptics, circa 1960, 2¾" x 1¾", **$10-$20**.

SWITCH PLATE COVER

Switch plate cover (in original package) portraying Richard Nixon as a comic hero with "N" on his shirt, "KaKaMaMie Co.," circa 1968, 4⅞" x 8¾", **$25-$35**.

AIR FRESHENER

Air freshener can with elephant image and reading "Republican BS Repellent" and "Spray immediately when republicans discuss inflation, taxes, crime, pollution, civil rights and why you should vote republican," "American Jetway Corp.," circa 1971, 2⅛" diameter, 6¾" high, **$15-$25**.

UTENSILS

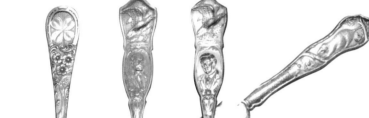

George Wallace double-blade pen-knife reading "Trust In The People 1976," "Barlow," 3⅜", **$20-$30**.

A spoon with William McKinley's image in the bowl, "Good Luck" on the front of the handle, and the reverse reading "Protection and Prosperity," circa 1896-1900; spoon with raised image of Charles Evan Hughes on handle, an eagle and "Hughes" down the handle, "Rodgers," circa 1916; similarly designed spoon, but with raised image of Woodrow Wilson and "Wilson" down the handle, "W R," circa 1916; and "Billy Possum" butter knife with raised image of a possum on the handle, circa 1908-'12. Billy Possum represented Taft, **$20-$25** each.

"For A Good Measure Of Good Government, Vote For Humphrey-Muskie" plastic teaspoon and tablespoon measurer, circa 1968, 5⅛", **$5-$10**.

Woodrow Wilson medal knife showcasing Wilson image and "Let Justice And Progress Go Hand In Hand" around border, circa 1913-'16, 1½" diameter, **$75-$125**.

Cast iron hatchet featuring embossed handle reading "All Nations Welcome But Carrie," referring to Carrie Nation, infamous for using a hatchet to destroy saloon property, circa early 20th century, 10½", **$35-$50**.

Double-blade aluminum penknife with image of George Washington and listing of presidents up to Herbert Hoover, circa 1928, 3⅜", **$25-$30**.

Money-holder pocketknife inscribed "Democratic National Convention/ Atlantic City/ 1964," "Imperial," 1¼" x 2⅛", **$15-$25**.

George McGovern-Thomas Eagleton pocketknife, circa 1972, 1½" diameter, value depends whether knife was made before Eagleton stopped being vice-presidential candidate.

"Ross Perot/ United We Stand" four-blade penknife in original box, also includes a 1⅝" campaign button with the candidate's image, "Cuttin Horse," circa 1992, 3⅜", **$30-$40**.

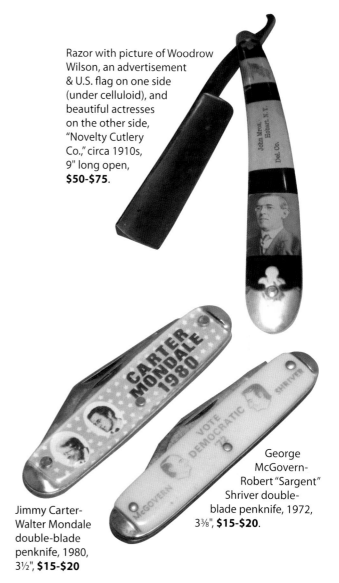

Razor with picture of Woodrow Wilson, an advertisement & U.S. flag on one side (under celluloid), and beautiful actresses on the other side, "Novelty Cutlery Co.," circa 1910s, 9" long open, **$50-$75**.

"Election 92 Collector's Edition" George H. W. Bush penknife in original packaging, "Case," circa 1992, 3", **$25-$35**.

Penknife given as a gift by Ronald Reagan with signature across the front, "Victorinox," circa 198-88, 3 7/8 " long open, **$35-$50**.

Jimmy Carter-Walter Mondale double-blade penknife, 1980, 3½", **$15-$20**

George McGovern-Robert "Sargent" Shriver double-blade penknife, 1972, 3⅜", **$15-$20**.

Knife sharpener with one edge reading "McKinley * Roosevelt," and the other side touting the virtues of being "Brave, Kind, Able, Honest," circa 1900, 1⅝" x 3⅜", ⅜" high, **$40-$60**.

FAN

"New Jersey For Bush-Quayle" card-board fan, wood handle, circa 1988-'92, 7⅞" x 12⅝", **$5-$10**.

THERMOMETER

Souvenir metal key embossed in Herbert Hoover's likeness and featuring a thermometer down the side, circa 1929-'32, 8¾", **$75-$100**.

CHIMNEY FLUE COVERS

During periods of warm weather, it was important to cover the unsightly chimney flue and prevent dirty air coming down and entering the room. Credible evidence has also been presented that these were automobile political plate attachments. Perhaps, they served many creative functions.

The following are four lithographic metal chimney flue covers, "S.S. Adams Co.," circa 1928, 8" diameter, **$75-$100** each.

"For President Herbert Hoover" blue-on-white flue cover.

"Hoover for President" black-on-white flue cover.

"For President Al Smith" blue-on-white flue cover.

"Smith for President" black-on-white flue cover.

TOILET PAPER

Toilet paper would not seem to be a useful campaign tool to express your candidate's positive qualities, but it has emerged as a humorous way to insult an opponent.

Anti-Dan Quayle unopened toilet paper roll picturing Quayle and reading "I Can Always Hide Behind The Bushes," circa 1988-'93, 4" diameter, 4½" high, **$10-$20**.

STORE AND SALOON DISPLAYS

Cardboard sign picturing William McKinley, "Compliments Of Liquid Peptonoids/ The Arlington Chem. Corp.," circa 1896-1900, 12¾" x 16¼", **$20-$30**.

Cardboard Atlantic & Pacific (A&P) Tea Co. store sign displaying Mrs. President Francis Folsom Cleveland. Reverse lists produce and product prices, circa 1887-'88/ 1893-'96, 10½" x 16½", **$50-$75**.

World War II die cut, aluminum foil and cardboard display box containing electric lighting system picturing Franklin Roosevelt in front of a U.S. flag and reading "We Will Win," circa 1940-'44, 16" x 4", 9" high, **$100-$150**.

Cardboard sign with colored portraits of Abraham Lincoln, George Washington and Theodore Roosevelt, "Sapolin Gold Enamel," circa 1901-'16, 16¼" x 9", **$20-$30**.

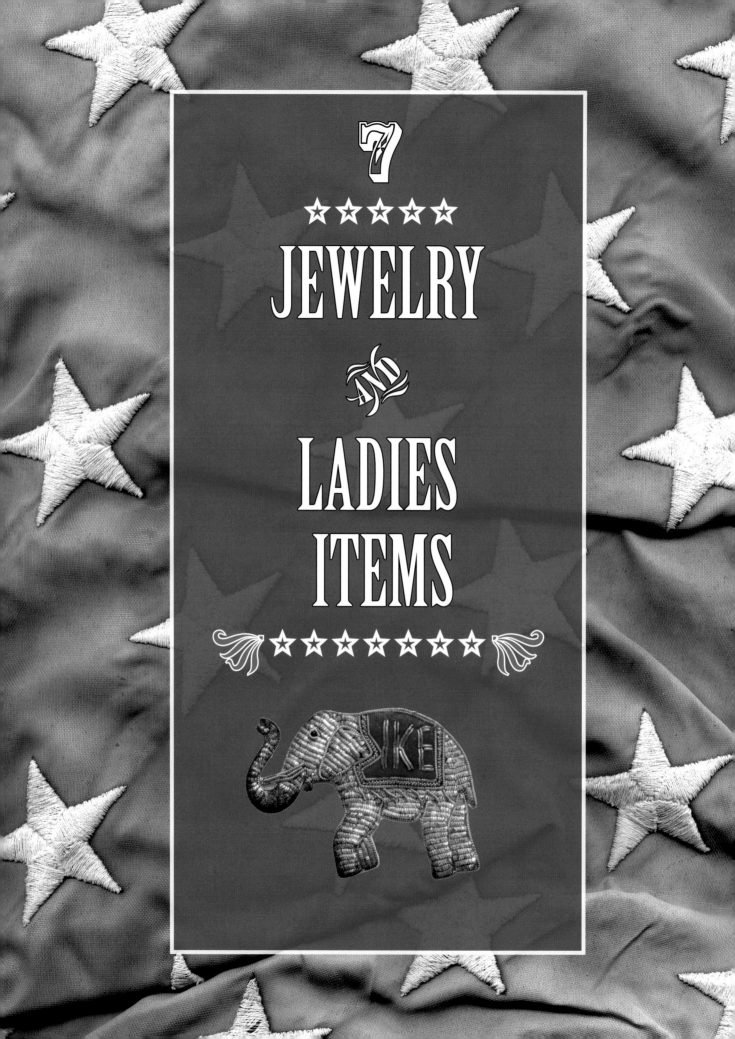

7

★ ★ ★ ★ ★

JEWELRY

and

LADIES

ITEMS

★ ★ ★ ★ ★ ★ ★ ★ ★

ampaign pieces sometimes had the dual purpose of being useful dress accessories.

During the 1950s and '60s, political jewelry was particularly popular.

BRACELETS

"IKE" bracelet with name surrounded by chain, disk attached, circa 1952-'56, 7" long, **$15-$25**.

"Nixon" faux-pearl bracelet and disk with politician's name and faux inset jewels, "OLEET," 7½" long, **$15-$25**.

"IKE" faux-pearl bracelet with brass cutout letter disk, circa 1952-'56, 7½" long, **$15-$25**.

"Nixon" brass letter bracelet and brass disk with Nixon's name and seal of California on reverse, circa 1960-'62, 7½" long, **$15-$25**.

Richard Nixon brass bracelet with brass elephant charm, enamel New Jersey charm and enamel charms spelling out "Nixon," circa 1960, 7¼" long, **$15-$25**.

"Kennedy" brass letter bracelet and brass donkey, circa 1960, 7" long, **$25-$40**.

"Campaign pieces sometimes had the dual purpose of being useful dress accessories."

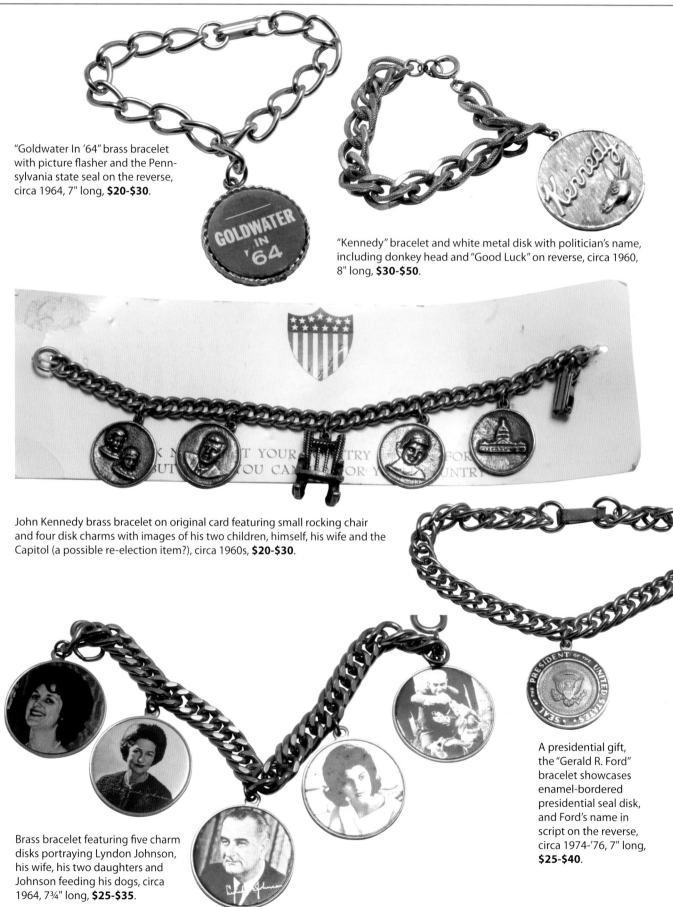

"Goldwater In '64" brass bracelet with picture flasher and the Pennsylvania state seal on the reverse, circa 1964, 7" long, **$20-$30**.

"Kennedy" bracelet and white metal disk with politician's name, including donkey head and "Good Luck" on reverse, circa 1960, 8" long, **$30-$50**.

John Kennedy brass bracelet on original card featuring small rocking chair and four disk charms with images of his two children, himself, his wife and the Capitol (a possible re-election item?), circa 1960s, **$20-$30**.

Brass bracelet featuring five charm disks portraying Lyndon Johnson, his wife, his two daughters and Johnson feeding his dogs, circa 1964, 7¾" long, **$25-$35**.

A presidential gift, the "Gerald R. Ford" bracelet showcases enamel-bordered presidential seal disk, and Ford's name in script on the reverse, circa 1974-'76, 7" long, **$25-$40**.

EARRINGS

"IKE" faux jewels imbedded into letters of earrings, circa 1952-'56, ¾" x ⅝", **$15-$20**.

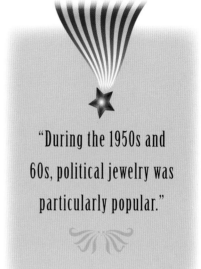

"During the 1950s and 60s, political jewelry was particularly popular."

"IKE," die cut brass letters on 1" diameter brass disk earrings, circa 1952-'56, **$15-$20**.

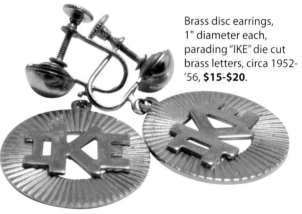

Brass disc earrings, 1" diameter each, parading "IKE" die cut brass letters, circa 1952-'56, **$15-$20**.

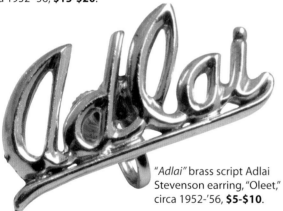

"*Adlai*" brass script Adlai Stevenson earring, "Oleet," circa 1952-'56, **$5-$10**.

"Nixon" on disk, silver colored earrings, circa 1960s, 1" diameter, **$10-$15**.

"Ike '56" metal earring with faux jewels imbedded in letters and number, "Oleet," circa 1956, 1" x ⅞", **$5-$10**.

BROACHES AND PINS

These are examples of broaches and pins for Adlai Stevenson's presidential campaigns, circa 1950s, **$10-$35** each.

Broaches and pins for Richard Nixon's presidential campaign, circa 1960 (unless noted otherwise), **$10-$30** each. The broach with Nixon's name in the center, surrounded by repeated wire circles, "WARNER," circa 1968, 1⅝" x 1⅜", **$10-$20**; and "Pat for First Lady" enamel-bordered brass broach, referring to Nixon's wife, circa 1968, 1¾" diameter, **$10-$20**.

Examples of broaches and pins for Dwight Eisenhower's presidential campaigns, circa 1950s, **$10-$25** each. A number of Eisenhower broaches were imported and made using silver- and/or brass-embroidered metallic threads, **$15-$30** each.

Broaches and pins for John Kennedy's presidential campaign, "Oleet," circa 1960, **$15-$30** each. The rocking-chair-shaped pin featuring faux-jewels insets signifies Kennedy's admission that a rocking chair relieved his back problems, circa 1961-'63, **$20-$30**.

PENDANTS

Six-sided brass pendant reading "Father Cox Jobless March Auxiliary Jan. 5, 1932." James Cox led a march of 25,000 unemployed Pennsylvanians to Washington and, for a time, he was a candidate for president on a Jobless Party ticket for public works and labor unions. Eventually, he decided to support Franklin Roosevelt for president, 7/8" x 7/8", **$35-$50**.

Six Richard Nixon and Nixon-Henry Cabot Lodge medal pendants (one with flasher), circa 1960, **$10-$20** each; and one Nixon-Spiro Agnew "1/20 10K GF" inauguration ball pendant, 1 1/8" square, **$25-$50**, apparently given as a gift.

John F. Kennedy-Lyndon B. Johnson silver profile pendant with reverse reading "Kennedy/ Inaugural Ball/ January 20, 1961/ Johnson," 7/8" diameter, **$50-$75**.

Three IKE and one Adlai brass pendants for Dwight D. Eisenhower and Adlai Stevenson, circa 1952-'56, 1½" diameter, **$10-$15** each. The design of the "I Like IKE" brass circular pendant with eagle image on blue enamel, 1¾" diameter, circular ridge lines and hole in the middle gives the pendant a phonograph record appearance.

John Fitzgerald Kennedy profile silver pendant with reverse reading "Democratic Party of Cook County/ Reception & dinner April 28, 1961 Richard J. Daley/ Chairman," 1" diameter, **$35-$50**.

Brass pendant featuring Lyndon Johnson photo and reverse reading "1965 Inauguration … ," 1¼" diameter, **$10-$15**.

Jack Kennedy faux-silver name pendant inset with nine faux, oval jewels, "Oleet," circa 1960, 1⅝" diameter, **$20-$30**.

"Barry" (Barry Goldwater) brass pendant showcasing an elephant wearing dark glasses, circa 1964, 1" diameter, **$10-$15**.

Metal pendant picturing Robert Kennedy and reverse featuring a peace sign, circa 1968, 1¼" diameter, **$15-$20**.

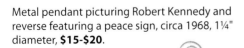

A presidential gift, the Jimmy Carter enamel-bordered, gold, presidential seal pendant features Carter's name in script on the reverse side, circa 1976-'80, ¾", **$30-$50**.

Brass pendant with John Kennedy photo attached, circa 1960, 1¼" diameter, **$20-$35**.

RINGS

From 1920 to 1955, inexpensive rings were often sold as visitor souvenirs, given away as product (cereal box) advertisements or purchased for box tops and 10 cents each as radio premiums. They were also made for the supporters of specific presidential candidates. The nostalgic and monetary values of such rings have grown significantly over the past decade.

"McKinley" horseshoe-nail ring with his image and name, circa 1896-1900, **$35-$65** .

"Hoover" metal ring, 1928, ½" x ¼", **$35-$50**.

"Hoover" brass and copper ring with elephant image, 1928, ½" diameter disk, **$35-$50**.

"Al Smith" metal ring, 1928, ½" x ¼", **$35-$50**.

Die cut metal ring with celluloid-covered oval picture of Al Smith inlaid in front, circa 1928, ¾" x ⅝", **$50-$75**.

"IKE" brass adjustable ring, circa 1952-'56, ½" diameter disk, **$15-$25**.

"Nixon '72" adjustable metal ring with stylized elephant, "John Roberts," 1972, ⅝" x ⅜", **$20-$25**.

Plastic flasher ring with faces of Mao Tse-tung and Richard Nixon, reading "President Nixon Visit To Peking 21st Feb. 1972," ⅝" diameter, **$20-$25**.

CUFF LINKS

James Blaine and John Logan photo cuff links, called "lever sleeve buttons," circa 1884, ⅞" diameter, **$100-$150**.

Elephants with black eyeglasses, cuff links on original card for Barry Goldwater, circa 1964, ¾" x ¾", **$20-$25**.

Apparently given as a gift, Richard Nixon cuff links with presidential seal and reverse reading "Richard Nixon 37th President," circa 1969-'73, ⅞" diameter, **$20-$30**.

"Nixon" circular brass cuff links with name embossed on dark blue enamel, circa 1968, ¾" diameter, **$10-$15**.

"Richard Nixon 37th President" cuff links in shape of a red, white and blue U.S. map, circa 1969-'73, ¾" x ½", **$10-$15**.

TIE TACKS

William J. Bryan celluloid tie tack, circa 1896-1900, **$35-$50**.

"Cleveland and Thurman" enameled brass tie tack with names on a horseshoe enclosing a four-leaf clover and "1888," **$35-$50**.

Grover Cleveland embossed die cut brass tie tack, circa 1888-'92, **$25-$40**.

Benjamin Harrison embossed die cut brass tie tack, circa 1888-'92, **$25-$40**.

Theodore Roosevelt photo tie tack embellished in filigree, oval brass frame, circa 1904, **$40-$50**.

Brass "gold bug" tie tack, circa 1896-1900, **$20-$30**.

"Free Silver" bug tie tack with ribbon, **$40-$50**.

Theodore Roosevelt photo tie tack embellished in filigree, round brass frame with U.S. flag, circa 1904, **$40-$50**.

Enameled brass tie tack of a bug wearing a top hat, carrying a cane and holding a bag of gold, circa 1896-1900, **$50-$75**.

Brass "Teddy Bear" tie tack symbolizing Theodore Roosevelt, **$15-$25**.

Theodore Roosevelt tie tack with his face poking through a Lincoln cent, circa 1910-'12, **$25-$35**.

Tie tack in the shape of Theodore Roosevelt's signature glasses, and Roosevelt's and Charles Fairbanks' photos in the lenses, circa 1904, 1⅜" wide, **$150-$200**.

"Cleveland" tie tack with name over a die cut X design, circa 1884-'92, **$35-$50**.

TIE CLIPS

It was more common than it is now for men to wear tie clips in the 1930s-'80s. Thousands of tie clips advertised businesses, products, clubs and associations, with many being political promotional devices. With a few exceptions, the tie clips illustrated are from the 1950s and '60s, and are valued at **$10-$35** each.

MONEY CLIPS

"IKE Golf Championship ... " on golf ball image, brass money clip, Dieges & Clust (?), ⅞" x 2⅛", 1955, **$15-$25**.

"Johnson for President" brass money clip with Lyndon B. Johnson's image on a blue plastic disk, "HIT," circa 1960-'64, 1⅝" x 2¼", **$15-$20**.

"During the 1880s, vest chain fobs featured glass-framed albumen pictures of candidates."

WATCHES

"Spiro Agnew Original" caricature watch, "D.T.C." (Dirty Times Co.), **$75-$100**; and Dan Quayle caricature watch, circa 1988-'92, **$25-$35**.

Undersell Dollar Watch advertisement on cardboard with crimped metal edge and picture of the "Dewey Model." William McKinley and Theodore Roosevelt are two of the prominent men pictured, circa 1899-1900, 1¾" diameter, **$20-$30**.

WATCH FOBS

In pre-wristwatch days, pocket watches and fobs were the means of telling time. Hanging outside the pocket, the fob made removing the watch easier. Collectors seek fobs because they often advertised machinery and other commercial products of the day, and often touted political support for certain candidates. During the 1880s, vest chain fobs featured glass-framed albumen pictures of candidates.

Brass fob with 1888 republican vice presidential candidate Levi Morton pictured under glass, and Benjamin Harrison shown on reverse side, circa 1888, ⅞" diameter, **$50-$75.**

Brass fob with 1884 republican vice presidential candidate John Logan pictured under glass, and James Blaine shown on reverse, circa 1884, 1" x 1½", **$50-$75.**

"Roosevelt/ 1904/ Fairbanks/ Washington," brass watch fob, 1¼" x 1⅜", **$30-$50.**

"Our Next President W.J. Bryan" white metal watch fob, "Jas. Matthews & Co.," circa 1908, 1⅜" x 1½", **$25-$40.**

"Our Choice Bryan & Kern/ 1908" copper watch fob, 1½" x 1¼", **$ 30-$50.**

Woodrow Wilson white metal watch fob, circa 1912-'16, 1⅜" x 1½", **$30-$40.**

Joseph G. Cannon (Speaker of the House of Representatives and presidential hopeful) brass watch fob, "J.H. Shaw," circa 1908, 1⅜" x 1½", **$25-$35.**

Woodrow Wilson copper watch fob with his image, a scale and the words "The Pen Is Mightier Than The Sword," circa 1916, 1¼" x 1¾", **$35-$50.**

Woodrow Wilson Inauguration copper watch fob with his image, shields and the words "Personal Escort/ Princeton Univ.," March 4, 1913, 1½" x 1⅝", **$50-$75.**

Four William H. Taft or Taft and James Sherman metal watch fobs, 1908, sizes vary slightly from 1⅜" x 1½", **$25-$40** each.

SEWING NEEDLES AND THIMBLES

After the 19ᵗʰ Amendment expanded women's suffrage throughout the country, the needle and thimble emerged as campaign tools directed toward the new voting constituents. Nowadays, most people are more inclined to toss a holed stocking into the trash than actually get a needle and thread to repair it. This was not the case during the 1920s.

Calvin Coolidge and Charles Dawes, Herbert Hoover and Charles Curtis, Alfred E. Smith, "Hoover*Home*Happiness" and "Vote The Straight Republican Ticket" thimbles, 1924 and 1928, **$15-$25** each.

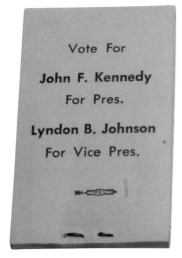

John F. Kennedy-Lyndon B. Johnson mending kit, 1⅝" x 2⅝", 1960, **$10-$15**.

"Eisenhower For President" mending kit, "Geiger Bros.," 1½" x 2⅛", circa 1952-'56, **$5-$10**.

Herbert Hoover-Charles Curtis jugate, cardboard needle mending kit, "The Keil & Styer Co.," 1928, 2¾" x 4¾", **$20-$25**.

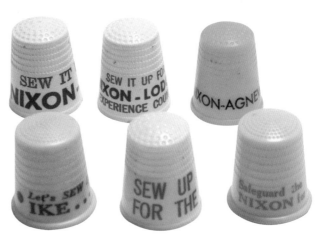

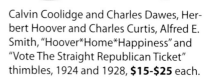

"Army And Navy Heroes Of Our Last War" cardboard needle mending kit with prominent pictures of William McKinley, Theodore Roosevelt and Adm. George Dewey, circa 1899-1900, 2⅝" x 4¾", **$10-$15**

Top left: "Sew It Up For Nixon–Lodge" thimble, circa 1960, ¾" diameter, ⅞" high, **$10-$15**. Top center: "Sew it up for Nixon–Lodge/ Experience Counts" thimble, circa 1960, ¾" diameter, ⅞" high, **$10-$15**. Top right: "Nixon-Agnew '72" thimble, 1972, ¾" diameter, ⅞" high, **$5-$10**. Bottom left: "Let's Sew It Up For IKE/ Vote Republican" thimble, circa 1952-'56, ¾" diameter, ⅞" high, **$10-$15**. Bottom center: "Sew Up Votes For The GOP" thimble, circa 1956-'60, ¾" diameter, ⅞" high, **$5-$10**. Bottom right: "Safeguard The American Home/ Nixon For U.S. Senator [California]" thimble, circa 1950s, ¾" diameter, ⅞" high, **$20-$30**.

POCKET MIRRORS

In addition to pin-back buttons, businesses frequently distributed advertising buttons with mirror on the backs. The popularity of pocket mirrors was at its height during first third of 20th century. On relatively rare occasions, pocket mirrors were made as part of a political campaign.

Adm. George Dewey pocket mirror, circa 1899-1900, 1¾", **$40-$50**.

"Pride Of New Jersey/ Woodrow Wilson" pocket mirror, 1912-'16, 1¾" diameter, **$300-$400**.

"Hoover/ Kean [for U.S. Senator] / Lawson [for New Jersey Governor]" circa 1928, 2" diameter, **$300-$400**.

"Goldwater In '64" gilt brass, enclosed flasher pocket mirror, 1964, 2½" diameter, **$10-$15**.

"I Like IKE," 1952-'56, 2⅛" diameter, **$15-$25**.

"Roosevelt" pocket mirror, circa 1936-'44, 3⅛" x 2⅛", **$25-$35**.

COMB AND NAIL FILE

"Nixon-Agnew" plastic comb and "Nixon Now" nail file, 1968-'72, **$5** each.

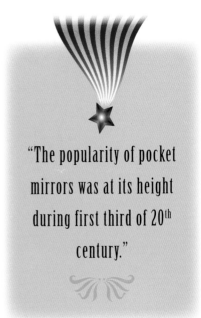

"The popularity of pocket mirrors was at its height during first third of 20th century."

LADIES' POWDER COMPACTS

Brass compact with 1⅜" celluloid of "Our Next President" Al Smith, 1928, 2¼" diameter, **$100-$150**.

"Kefauver for Pres." brass powder compact including a 2" Estes Kefauver (presidential hopeful and 1956 democratic vice-presidential candidate) picture button, "Chase," 1952-'56, 2¾" diameter, **$75-$100**.

Square, brass, red, white and blue enamel powder compact touting "Willkie," "Fifth/Rex/Avenue," 1940, 2⅞" x 2⅞", **$50-$60**.

"Taft for President" brass powder compact with 2" Robert Taft picture button, "Chase," 1952, 2¾" diameter, **$50-$75**.

PURSE

"We Want Willkie" circular brass powder compact, Mary Lewis Distributor, 1940, 2½2⅞" diameter, **$50-$60**.

Simulated-leather lady's purse featuring a multicolor cloth picture of a bejeweled Jackie Kennedy with John Kennedy in the background, circa 1960-'63, 10½2⅞" x 4½2⅞", 12¼42⅞" high, **$35-$50**. This purse clearly emphasizes Jackie Kennedy. When was it made? Was John Kennedy still alive? Sometimes, items create more questions than answers.

8

★ ☆ ★ ★ ★ ☆ ★

TOYS

AND

HANDMADE ITEMS

✦ ★ ★ ★ ★ ★ ★ ★ ★ ✦

ames and toys have long been important parts of home entertainment. Checkers, board games, jigsaw puzzles and other toys would keep the children, as well as the growing leisure class, occupied.

Over the past several decades, collecting old toys, especially in their original boxes, has grown enormously in popularity, and thus, the items have increased in value. This has both increased the cost of old political toys and encouraged the production of new ones.

"Old board games are collected today because of their great cover graphics and references to past personalities."

CHECKERS

The white checkers are pressed wooden images of democrats Grover Cleveland and Thomas Hendricks, while the black checkers are republicans James Blaine and John Logan. The last names of each pair are on the reverse, circa 1884, **$40-60** each checker, or an entire set valued at **$400-$600**.

BOARD GAMES

Old board games are popularly collected today because of their great cover graphics and references to real and imagined personalities of the past.

"The Rough Riders" board game showing a charging Theodore Roosevelt on the cover, Parker Brothers, circa 1899-1904, 10½" x 20½", rare.

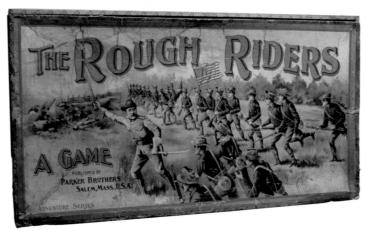

"The Kennedy Game" board game features John Kennedy and his extended family on the cover. Their faces appear carved for posterity in a Mount Rushmore pose, Harrison and Winter, Inc., circa 1962, 9¾" x 19¼", **$50-$70**.

"Meet the Presidents" board game, which has been updated frequently throughout the years. This one has a 1950 copyright and includes aluminum presidential coins beginning with George Washington and up to Harry Truman, Selchow & Righter Co., circa 1950-'52, 10" x 15", **$35-$50**. Technically, though never likely, Truman could have constitutionally run for a third presidential term in 1952, since the 22nd Amendment limiting terms was passed during his presidency and did not apply to him.

"Who Can Beat Nixon" board game illustrates the personalities, issues and possible tactics of the period, Harrison-Blaine, circa 1970-'72, 8¾" x 11½", **$35-$50**.

JIGSAW PUZZLES

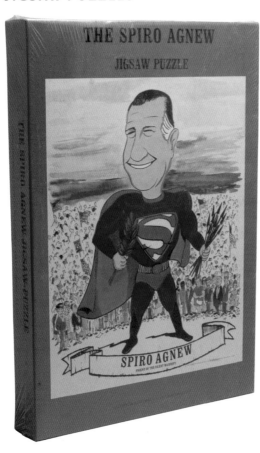

"This Is A Two-Faced Jigsaw Puzzle" with caricature of Richard Nixon on one side of the puzzle, and on the other side, a caricaturized Spiro Agnew implying his desire for censorship, "The Puzzle Factory," circa 1970, 8¼" x 12⅛", **$20-$30**.

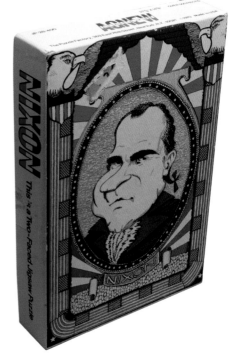

"The Spiro Agnew" jigsaw puzzle depicting Agnew as Superman, Gameophiles Unlimited, Inc., circa 1970, 9¼" x 13", **$20-$25**.

OTHER PUZZLES

"16 to 1 Puzzle" consisting of two solid-iron pieces: a 2" diameter metal disk (originally silver in color) and featuring a maze-like indentation on each side; and a gold (now faded) 1¾" x 1⅞" iron disk held by the disk maze. The object of the game is for the participant to free the gold disk from the silver disk by working through the maze, circa 1896-1900, **$100-$200**.

"Teddy And The Lion" cardboard puzzle with spinning disk in order to determine "Which Black Man Turns Into a Yellow Lion?," "Sam Loyd," circa 1910-'12, **$100-$150**.

CHILD'S PLAY TOYS

William Taft celluloid toy with metal wheels, circa 1908-'12, 1" x 1¾", rare. The bottom of the Taft figure is weighted so that the figure remains upright when the toy is rolling.

Jimmy Carter wind-up, plastic, walking peanut toy with Carter's caricaturized face on the peanut, circa 1976-80, "B. J. Wolfe Ent.," 4⅝" high, **$25-$35**.

Dwight Eisenhower battery-operated mechanical elephant holding an "I Like IKE" flag with its trunk and wearing a red, embroidered "I Like IKE" blanket, Line MAR Toys (Japan), circa 1952-'56, 10" x 5", 6½" high, **$100-$150**; and a smaller wind-up mechanical elephant, complete with two "IKE" buttons attached to its red blanket, "Modern Toys" (Japan), circa 1952-'56, 5" x 2⅛", 3½" high, **$25-$45**.

CLICKERS

"Click with Dick," "Click with Dick/ Nixon for President" and "Veterans For Nixon" metal clickers, circa 1960s, **$10-$25** each.

PHONOGRAPH RECORD

33 1/3 RPM record with excerpts from Nixon's 1968 nomination acceptance speech, mailed as a postcard requesting support and donations, "Auravision," circa 1968, 6⅞" square, **$15-$20**.

Two "Political Squiggle Jiggles" motorized pens in original packaging, caricatures of Bill Clinton and Ross Perot, "Hart Enterprises, Inc.," circa 1993, 9¼", **$15-$25** each.

MUSIC BOX

"IKE" brass windup music box inlaid with fake jewels, circa 1952-'56, 1⅛" x 1¼", **$15-$25**.

Three lithographic colored metal toys featuring candidates that move back and forth when the lower metal straps are squeezed, "Schylling," 3¼" x 6½", **$15-$25** each. They include Robert Dole and William Clinton in suits and bowties, circa 1996; John Kerry and George W. Bush in suits, circa 2004; and George W. Bush and John Kerry as boxers, circa 2004.

WHISTLE

"Landon & Knox" aluminum whistle, circa 1936, 1" high, **$20-$30**.

DECKS OF CARDS

All the following card decks are 2¼" x 3½" or slightly larger unless otherwise noted.

"I Like IKE" double deck of playing cards, "ARRCO Playing Card Co.," circa 1952-'56, 3⅞" x 4¾", **$30-$50**.

"Kennedy Kards" picturing caricature of John Kennedy on cover, as well as his relatives and Lyndon B. Johnson on card backs and face cards, "Humor House, Inc.," circa 1963, **$25-$40**.

"Politicards" with Jimmy Carter caricature on the cover of the box, and portraying caricatures of the period's political activists on the cards themselves, Politicards, Inc., circa 1980, **$10-$20**.

"Politicards" with Richard Nixon caricature on the cover of the box, and portraying caricatures of the period's political activists on the cards themselves, Politicards, Inc., circa 1971-'72, **$15-$25**.

"1972 Presidential Campaign Commemorative Issue" card deck with George McGovern as the Joker, de Ville, **$10-$20**.

"Decision '92" cards presenting all the candidates and issues leading to the 1992 presidential election, "AAA Sports, Inc.," 5⅝" x 8¾", **$20-$30**.

PUPPETS

Two similar caricature Ronald Reagan plastic hand puppets that throw arms and hands forward as though boxing, one in blue cloth, the other in red, white and blue cloth, "ROJUS," circa 1980-'88, 12" high, **$25-$35** each.

Two rubber hand puppets caricaturizing William Clinton and Robert Dole, Mask Illusions, 1996, 10¾" high, **$20-$30 each**. By placing a hand within one of the rubber puppets, the user can move the head, facial features and mouth in funny or grotesque ways.

DIE AND GAMBLING CHIP

"Hoover Wins/ 1928" irregular-shaped clear plastic, red-dotted die with small dice inside, 1" diameter, **$30-$40**.

Yellow gambling chip with charging Rough Rider image, associated with Theodore Roosevelt, 1⅜" diameter, **$15-$20**.

MAGIC LIGHT BULB

Ronald Reagan supporters at the 1968 Republican National Convention used magic light bulbs that looked like ordinary bulbs but with batteries to light bulbs when desired. Attached to each bulb was a paper reading "Ron Turns Me On." When the hall lights dimmed, hundreds of hands held the light bulbs high for dramatic effect, circa 1968, 4¼" high, **$25-$40**.

DOLLS

With the steady popularity of dolls, there has been a growing production of presidential and presidential candidate dolls. Frequently they are humorous caricatures, but sometimes they honor, or at least are neutral toward, the candidates.

Barry Goldwater presidential campaign doll in original display box, specially made for car dashboards, "Remco," circa 1964, 5⅛" x 3¼", 7⅛" high, **$25-$40**.

Lyndon B. Johnson presidential campaign doll in original display box, specially made for car dashboards, "Remco," circa 1964, 5⅛" x 3¼", 7⅛" high, **$25-$40**.

Ronald Reagan caricature doll with plastic head, stuffed cloth body and plastic stand, circa 1980-'88, 12" high, **$25-$35**; and a George H.W. Bush caricature doll with plastic head and stuffed cloth body, circa 1988-'92, 11¼" high, **$20-$30**.

Cloth-filled and printed Ronald Reagan doll in original box, critical of his "Supply Side Reaganomics," and with the other side portraying a poor man wearing a barrel, circa 1981-'88, **$25- $35**.

George H.W. Bush doll in original display box, part of a set also honoring Gen. Colin Powell and Gen. Norman Schwarzkopf, "In Time Products, Inc.," circa 1991, 4" x 3" box, **$20-$30**.

George W. Bush talking doll in original display box with actual speech sound bites if back button is pushed, "talkingpresidents.com," circa 2002, 2½" x 6", 15¾" high, **$20-$30**.

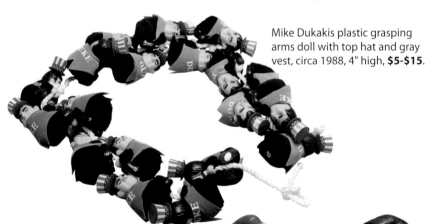

Mike Dukakis plastic grasping arms doll with top hat and gray vest, circa 1988, 4" high, **$5-$15**.

Two grasping-arms plastic boxer dolls: George H.W. Bush in blue cloth and Mike Dukakis donning red, circa 1988, 4" high, **$5-15** each.

"Uptown," William Clinton plastic and cloth suited doll with saxophone, moves and emits music when button on stand is pressed, 14½" high, **$25-$40**.

SCATOLOGICAL ADULT HUMOR

Two lighthearted, humorous, plastic and cloth, towel-donning dolls: Jimmy Carter, circa 1976-'80 and Richard Nixon, circa 1972-'74, 7" high, **$20-$30** each.

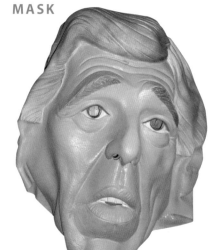

PAPER DOLLS

"First Family Paper doll & Cut-out Book," including paper dolls of Ronald and Nancy Reagan and two of their children, and 16 color pages filled with outfits, 1981, 9" x 12", **$15-$25**.

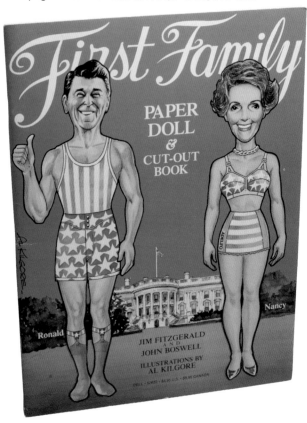

MASK

Since Halloween is so close to elections, it should not be surprising that presidential masks were popular, yet they were usually distorted exaggerations of presidents, not contenders. This 2004 John Kerry mask is an exception, circa 2004, 8½" x 11", **$20-$25**.

JACK-IN-THE-BOX

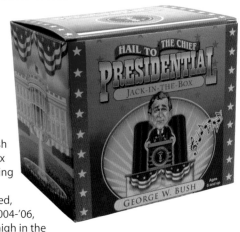

George W. Bush jack-in-the-box has him popping out when the handle is turned, "DMA," circa 2004-'06, 5½" x 6⅝", 6" high in the box, **$25-$35**.

COMIC DISPLAY PIECE

Black-on-white plastic caricature of Spiro Agnew, circa 1968-'72, 10¾" high, **$15-$25**.

BANKS

Civilian Dwight D. Eisenhower metal bank, "Banthrico Inc.," circa 1952-'60, 3½" x 2⅜" base, 5⅜" high, **$25- $35**.

Dwight Eisenhower in uniform metal bank, "Banthrico Inc.," circa 1945-'52, 2¼" x 1⅝" base, 5 ½" high, **$25-$35**.

"F.D. Roosevelt" metal bank, circa 1930s, 3" x 2⅛", 4⅞" high, **$35-$50**.

"F.D. Roosevelt" metal bank, circa 1930s, 2⅜" x 3¼", 5¼" high, **$35-$50**.

HANDMADE PIECES

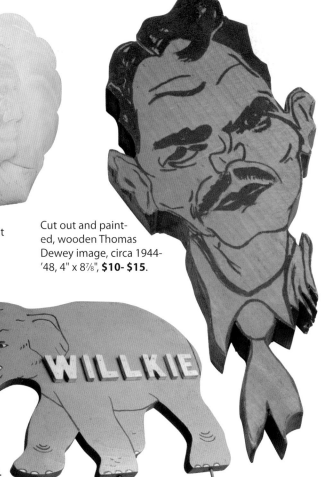

Carved Franklin Roosevelt image on a shell, circa 1933-'44, 7" x 7", rare.

Cut out and painted, wooden Thomas Dewey image, circa 1944-'48, 4" x 8⅞", **$10- $15**.

Thomas Dewey image carved onto "Ivory Soap" bar and then painted, with the reverse showing original "Ivory" soap bar, circa 1940s, 2¾" x 4¼", **$20-$25**.

"Willkie" hand-cut wooden elephant sign, circa 1940, 11" x 17½", **$30 -$50**.

9

⭐ ⭐ ⭐ ⭐ ⭐

CLOCKS, LAMPS

and

AUTOMOTIVE ITEMS

⭐ ⭐ ⭐ ⭐ ⭐ ⭐ ⭐ ⭐ ⭐

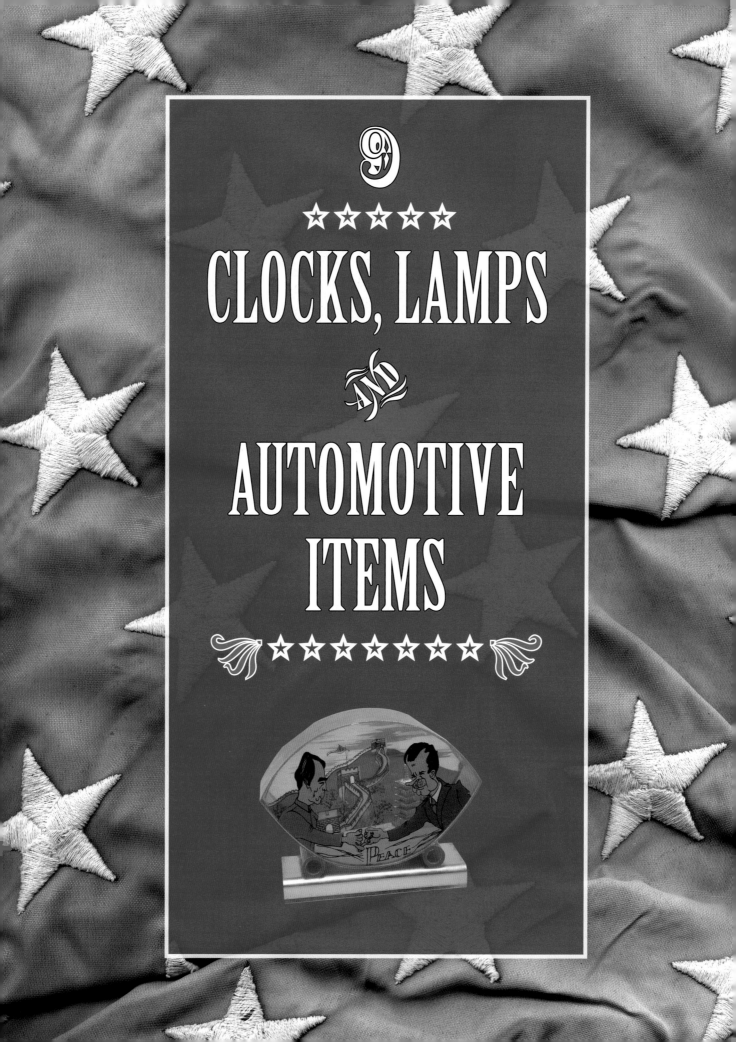

CLOCKS

Clock and metal lamp, missing glass cover and lighthouse bulb, symbolizing Franklin Roosevelt standing by lighthouse to safely guide the Ship of State, "Oxford Self Starting," mid 1930s, 4⅝" x 14" wooden base, **$35-$50**.

Two variations of an embossed-metal Theodore Roosevelt statuette on horseback. One piece has a circular cutout to hold a clock (clock missing), and the other (top) is a solid example, circa 1899-1901, 2¼" x 8¼" base, 10¾" high, **$150-$200** each.

During the 1930s, a variety of clocks embedded in metal statues were produced in favor of Franklin Delano Roosevelt.

"F.D.R. The Man of the Hour" clock with Franklin D. Roosevelt calmly steering the Ship of State, "United Clock Corp.," circa mid 1930s, 4¼" x 10" base, 15" high, **$100-$150**.

"Roosevelt/ at the Wheel For A New Deal" clock, "Gibraltar Electric Clock Co., Inc.," circa mid 1930s, 3¾" x 9¼", **$100-$150**.

"Steersmen of the U.S.A." colored clock depicting Franklin D. Roosevelt at the helm of a ship, hands on the wheel, and positioned on either side of him are George Washington and Abraham Lincoln, "United Clock Corp.," mid 1930s, 5" x 11½", 14½" high, **$150-$200**.

"The Spirit Of The U.S.A." clock, including green and red light bulbs and featuring Franklin D. Roosevelt bust at the top, Secretary of Labor Frances Perkins on bottom right and retired Gen. H. S. Johnson, N. R. A. director, on bottom left. Clock face has night club image with bartender's hands and arms shaking a cocktail, circa 1933-'35, "United Clock Corp.," 3¾" x 9½" base, 10½" high, **$175-$250**.

The "Sunflower" clock features a young lady holding a sunflower with more sunflowers at her feet. It appears to favor Alf Landon's 1936 presidential effort since the sunflower was his campaign symbol, "United Electric Co.," circa mid 1930s, 8" x 4 ½" base, 11 ½" high, **$150-$200**.

Glass-enclosed clock with White House image, mounted on a metal plate with rim picturing all the presidents up to Lyndon B. Johnson, circa 1963-'66, 10" diameter, **$20-$30**.

Clock mounted on Spiro Agnew caricature button, "Lendan," circa 1969-'73, 9" diameter, **$50-$100**.

Clock presumably shows Franklin D. Roosevelt and Vice President John Garner steering the Ship of State, Sessions Clock Co., circa mid 1930s, 3⅞" x 11" base, 12½" high, **$100-$150**.

LAMPS

"F. D. R. The Man of the Hour" metal lamp with Franklin D. Roosevelt steering the Ship of State, circa mid 1930s, 3⅛" x 6¾" base, 14½" high, **$200-$300**.

"Time to Drink" metal lamp and clock depicting celebration of prohibition's end, Gibraltar Electric Clock Co., circa 1933-'36, 3" x 9" base, 17½" high, **$100-$150**.

"Peace" glass and plastic lamp portraying Richard Nixon shaking pinky fingers with Communist China Premier Cho En La, circa 1972, 2⅜" x 6" metal base, 5½" high, **$30-$40**.

METAL SIGNS

"Herbert Hoover" aluminum sign with realistic painted picture ,
1928-'32, 14" x 4", **$30-$40**.

"Hoover" metal oval sign, 1928-'32,
5⅝" x 3⅝", **$15-$20**.

TRANSISTOR RADIO

Jimmy Carter transistor radio featuring
a toothy Carter with top hat and peanut
body, 1976-'80, 3" diameter x 7" high,
$15-$25.

SUCTION CUPS

Rubber suction cups were another
way to apply something to an inside
car window.

"Landon/ Knox" die cut, yellow,
cardboard sunflower with rubber suction
cup, 1936, 4½" diameter, **$15-$20**; and
"Willkie/ McNary" yellow cardboard with
rubber suction cup, 1940, 4½" diameter,
$10-$15.

*"Partisan support was
expressed by attaching
politically oriented metal
plates to cars."*

MARCHING TORCHES

From 1860-1890, torchlight political parades were a major part of any entertaining, evening-time political rally. The kerosene-filled torches were designed to swivel during lengthy parades. In his booklet *Political Campaign Torches*, Smithsonian Institution, Washington, D.C., 1964, Herbert R. Collins traced and identified 19th-century campaign torches.

Illustrated are several examples of torch variations with date estimations based on Collins' patent and other research, **$40-$60** each.

> "From 1860-1890, torchlight political parades were a major part of any entertaining, evening-time political rally."

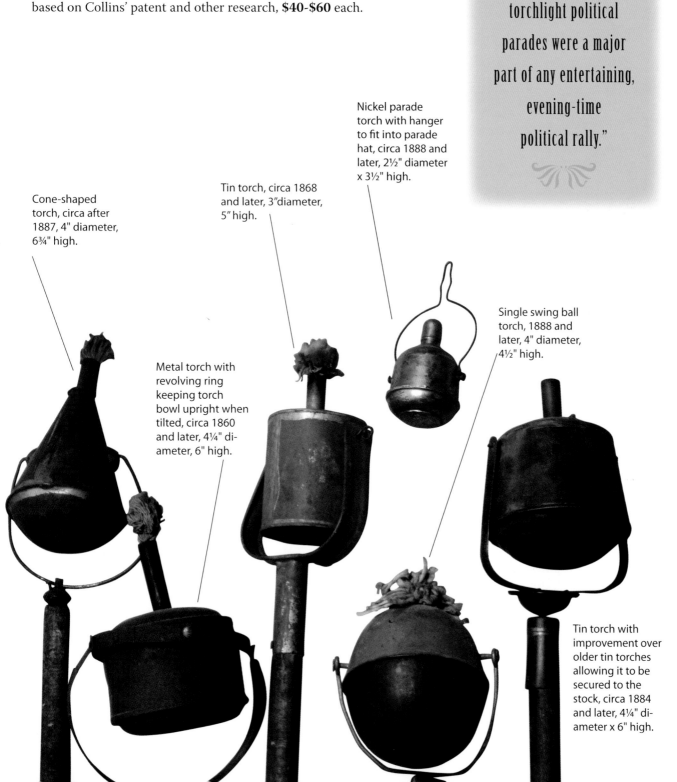

Cone-shaped torch, circa after 1887, 4" diameter, 6¾" high.

Tin torch, circa 1868 and later, 3"diameter, 5" high.

Nickel parade torch with hanger to fit into parade hat, circa 1888 and later, 2½" diameter x 3½" high.

Metal torch with revolving ring keeping torch bowl upright when tilted, circa 1860 and later, 4¼" diameter, 6" high.

Single swing ball torch, 1888 and later, 4" diameter, 4½" high.

Tin torch with improvement over older tin torches allowing it to be secured to the stock, circa 1884 and later, 4¼" diameter x 6" high.

AUTOMOBILE POLITICAL PLATES

As an increasing number of people bought and drove automobiles during the 1920s, partisan support was expressed by attaching politically oriented metal plates to cars. By the 1950s, it was much easier and cheaper to use bumper stickers.

"Al Smith For President" metal plate, 1928, 4⅜" x 11⅞", **$35-$50**.

"LaFollette For President" plate designed for 1924 Progressive Party candidate Robert LaFollette, 2¾" x 11⅞", **$50-$75**.

"1936/ Forward with Roosevelt" metal plate for Franklin Roosevelt, 4½" x 11½", **$30-$40**.

"All the Way With LBJ" metal plate for Lyndon Johnson, 1964, 6" x 12", **$20-$25**.

"Texas/ LBJ For The USA" plastic red, white and blue flasher plate for Lyndon Johnson, 1964, 3" x 6", **$15-$25**.

Five metal license plates for Herbert Hoover, 1928-'32, **$40-60** each.

Wendell Willkie metal plate, circa 1940, 3¾" x 13½", **$25-$35**.

"I Like IKE" metal plate with trumpeting, enthusiastic elephant, 1952-'56, 5¾" x 11", **$30-$50**.

"California/ BARRY" miniature license plate for Barry Goldwater, 1964, 2¼" x 4", **$15-$25**.

"Landon" white lettering on blue ribbon applied to red reflector plate, 1936, 3⅜" diameter, **$30-$40**.

Independent Party candidate George Wallace metal plates, 1968, 6" x 12", **$10-$20**. By this time, metal plates had long since given way to the much cheaper bumper stickers.

A Herbert Hoover picture-and-name reflector with mirror, 1928-'32, 2⅛" x 8", 2½" high, **$150-$200**; and a miniature Hoover name reflector pin, circa 1928-'32, 1½" long, **$35-$50**.

DECALS AND WINDOW STICKERS

As opposed to stamps and stickers placed on opaque objects, decals and window stickers were applied to inside windows where they were protected from the elements. How many have survived?

"Roosevelt Appreciator League" decal for the 1936 Roosevelt Round-up Rally, 5" x 5¼", **$25-$40**.

Two 1936 Alf Landon and Frank Knox decals: a brown and yellow sunflower decal, 4½" diameter, **$15-$20**; and a tan covered wagon decal, 4" x 5⅜", **$20-$30**.

"Forward with Stevenson" window sticker, circa 1952-'56, 3" x 7½", **$10-$15**.

"I Like IKE" decal picturing Dwight D. Eisenhower, circa 1952-'60, 3⅛" x 4¾", **$5-$10**.

Two 1940 Wendell Willkie decals: a "Willkie" red, white and blue decal, 2⅛" x 8⅜", **$10-$15**; and a "No Third Term! /Democrats For Willkie" decal with Uncle Sam pointing thumbs down, 4" x 8", **$15-$20**.

John F. Kennedy/ Lyndon B. Johnson window sticker, 1960, 3¼" x 8¼", **$10-$15**.

"Dewey" red, white and blue decal, Metalart Corp., circa 1944-'48, 1⅝" x 7¾", **$5-$10**; and an "All 48 In '48/ Dewey-Warren" sticker, 1948, 3⅞" diameter, **$5-$15**.

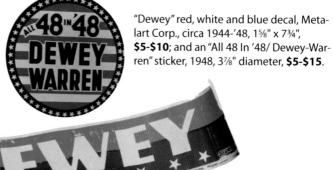

Richard Nixon/ Henry Cabot Lodge window sticker, Aldine, 1960, 4" x 5½", **$5-$10**.

POLITICAL CONVENTION LICENSE PLATE

"Democratic National Convention" official New Jersey license plate, for the 1964 Atlantic City Convention, 6" x 12", **$50-$75**.

INAUGURATION LICENSE PLATES

These are official license plates used during the Washington, D.C., Presidential Inauguration festivities.

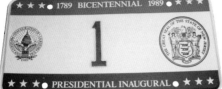

Two "1789 Bicentennial 1989 /Presidential Inaugural" plates for George H.W. Bush/ Dan Quayle Inaugural, 6⅛" x 12", plate "NJ-1" and plate "1" with New Jersey State Seal, **$40-$60** each.

"District of Columbia Inauguration 1973" plate for Richard Nixon/ Spiro Agnew Inaugural, 6" x 12", **$25-$45**.

"Presidential Inauguration Committee 1973 Official Vehicle" card, 4" x 11", and the "1973 Inaugural Registration Certificate," **$30-$50** for both.

"An American Journey/ Building a Bridge To The 21st Century" plate "NJ 1" for Bill Clinton/ Al Gore Inaugural, 1997, 6⅛" x 12", **$40-$60**.

"An American Reunion" plate "1-NJ" for Bill Clinton/ Al Gore Inaugural, 1993, 6⅛" x 12", **$40-$60**.

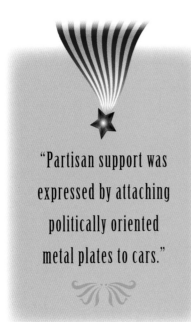

"Partisan support was expressed by attaching politically oriented metal plates to cars."

INAUGURATION PARKING SIGN

Washington, D.C., no parking sign used during Richard Nixon's Inauguration Day celebration, 1969, 12" x 18", **$50-$100**.

BUMPER STICKERS

During the past 50 years, the bumper sticker has arguably emerged as the nation's most popular political advertisement. Yet, how many unused ones survived the 1950s and the 1960 elections?

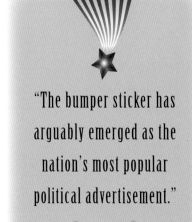

Two 1960 Nixon stickers: "Nixon-Lodge," 2" x 7¼"; and "I'm a Democrat for Nixon," 7¼" x 1⅞", **$5-$10** each.

"The bumper sticker has arguably emerged as the nation's most popular political advertisement."

"IKE and Dick/ Jersey Says Yes!" bumper sticker, circa 1952-'56, 3¾" x 9", **$10-$15**; and "All Those In Favor Say IKE" bumper sticker, "Emress Specialty Co.," circa 1952-'56, 4" x 8⅞", **$10-$15**.

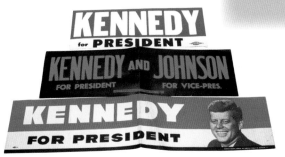

"Stevenson/Kefauver" bumper sticker, Aldine Co., 1956, 3⅞" x 15", **$10-$15**.

Three 1960 John Kennedy stickers: "Kennedy For President," 10⅜" x 3⅞"; "Kennedy for President and Johnson For Vice-Pres.," Novelty Printing Co., 13⅞" x 4"; and "Kennedy for President" with picture of Kennedy, 17⅝" x 3⅞", **$10-$25** each.

CAR OR HOUSE DOOR HANDLE ATTACHMENTS

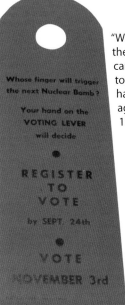

"Whose finger will trigger the next Nuclear Bomb?" cardboards with holes at top for placing on door handles as a scare tactic against Barry Goldwater, 1964, 3½" x 10½", **$3-$5**.

"No Third Term" anti-Franklin Roosevelt third term, unhappy Uncle Sam cardboard with string attached for door handle hanging, circa 1940, 3⅜" diameter, **$5-$10**.

10

★ ★ ★ ★ ★

OFFICE

&

SCHOOL ITEMS

★ ★ ★ ★ ★ ★ ★ ★ ★

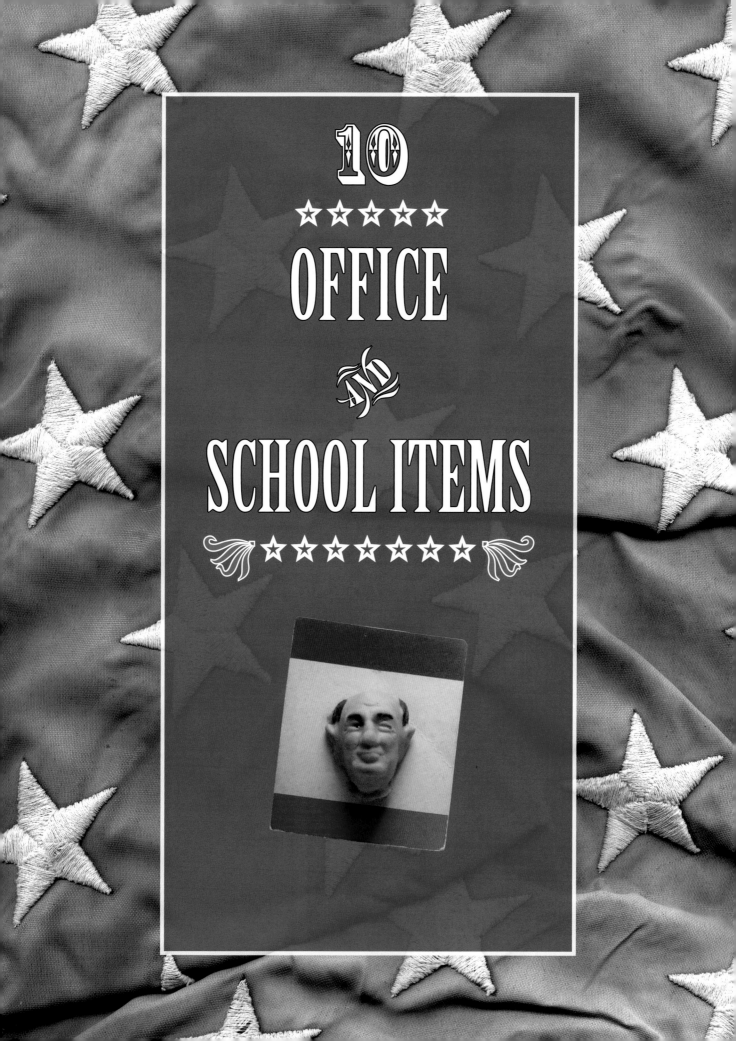

PENCIL HOLDERS

Presidents and their terms in office, blue plastic pencil holder listing presidents up in office until the term of John Kennedy, circa 1961, "Sterling S P CO," 7¾" x 3¾", **$10-$20**.

Herbert Hoover/ Charles Curtis dark-green "Our Chief Commanders" pencil holder with faded gold printing, circa 1928-'32, 10⅝" x 5 ⅝", **$30-$50**.

PENS

"Free Silver, 1896 Democratic Campaign Souvenir/ Wm. Jennings Bryan for President/ Arthur Sewall for Vice President" glass tube pen with words on enclosed silver-colored paper, 5¾" long and protected by a 6¼" wooden tube, **$100-$150**.

"We Want IKE For President" plastic and brass ball-point pen, circa 1950s, 5⅛" long, **$20-$25**.

"Goldwater-Miller" plastic ball-point pen, 1964, 5" long, **$10-$20**.

Richard Nixon brass ball-point pen with signature, circa 1968-'73, 5¼" long, **$10-$20**.

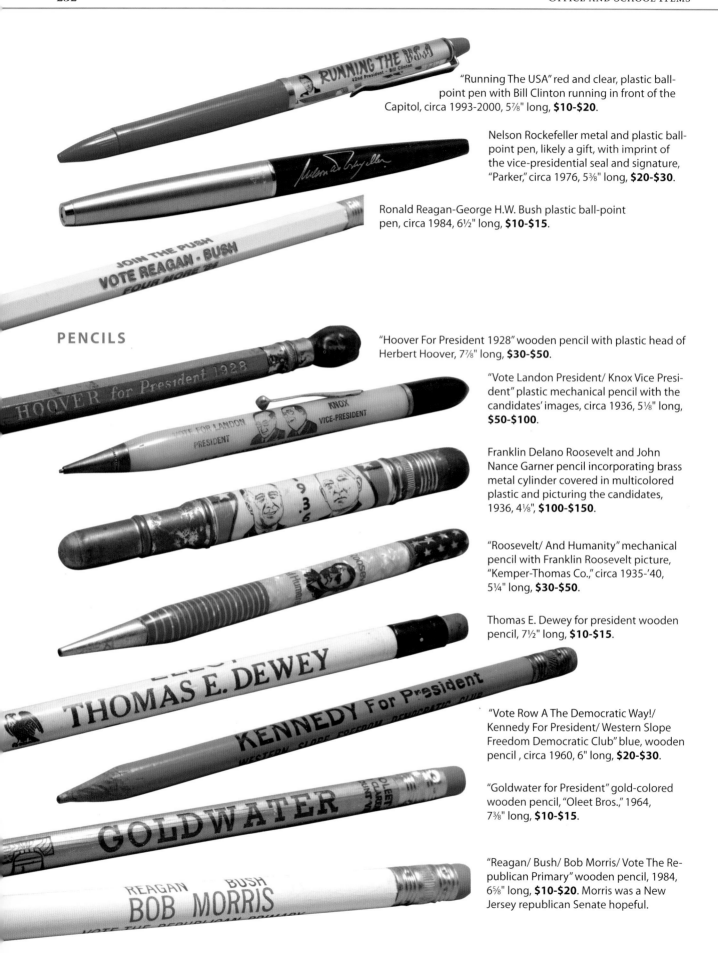

"Running The USA" red and clear, plastic ball-point pen with Bill Clinton running in front of the Capitol, circa 1993-2000, 5⅞" long, **$10-$20**.

Nelson Rockefeller metal and plastic ball-point pen, likely a gift, with imprint of the vice-presidential seal and signature, "Parker," circa 1976, 5⅜" long, **$20-$30**.

Ronald Reagan-George H.W. Bush plastic ball-point pen, circa 1984, 6½" long, **$10-$15**.

PENCILS

"Hoover For President 1928" wooden pencil with plastic head of Herbert Hoover, 7⅞" long, **$30-$50**.

"Vote Landon President/ Knox Vice President" plastic mechanical pencil with the candidates' images, circa 1936, 5⅛" long, **$50-$100**.

Franklin Delano Roosevelt and John Nance Garner pencil incorporating brass metal cylinder covered in multicolored plastic and picturing the candidates, 1936, 4⅛", **$100-$150**.

"Roosevelt/ And Humanity" mechanical pencil with Franklin Roosevelt picture, "Kemper-Thomas Co.," circa 1935-'40, 5¼" long, **$30-$50**.

Thomas E. Dewey for president wooden pencil, 7½" long, **$10-$15**.

"Vote Row A The Democratic Way!/ Kennedy For President/ Western Slope Freedom Democratic Club" blue, wooden pencil , circa 1960, 6" long, **$20-$30**.

"Goldwater for President" gold-colored wooden pencil, "Oleet Bros.," 1964, 7⅜" long, **$10-$15**.

"Reagan/ Bush/ Bob Morris/ Vote The Republican Primary" wooden pencil, 1984, 6⅝" long, **$10-$20**. Morris was a New Jersey republican Senate hopeful.

"President Nixon/ Now More Than Ever" wooden pencil, circa 1972, 7⅜" long, **$5-$10**.

George H.W. Bush/ Dan Quayle wooden pencil, circa 2000, 7⅜", **$5**.

ERASER

Adlai Stevenson figural rubber eraser on original card, made to attach to a pencil or place in a jacket lapel hole for display, 1¼", **$20-$25**.

"One dared not fold or cover any recently signed letter without first applying a blotter."

BLOTTERS

Before the emergence and dominance of the ball-point pen, one dared not fold or cover any recently signed letter without first applying a blotter. Not surprisingly, blotters were given away as political endorsements or advertisements.

"Leading Our Fight To Victory" blotter with portraits of Franklin Delano Roosevelt and other World War II allies, Fidelity Federal, circa 1942-'44, 9" x 4", **$10-$20**; and a blotter with George Washington and Herbert Hoover images, as well as the assertion that if Washington could speak, he would say Hoover "has in every way inculcated the principles for which I lived and died," circa 1932, 9" x 4", **$15-$25**.

RULER

"Farmer Henry Krajewski" metal ruler for Poor Man's Party candidate for president, advocating no income tax in 1953 if a citizen, 55 years of age or older, had less than $6,000 in annual income and Social Security retirement, circa 1952, 12⅜" x 2", **$20-$30**.

LETTER OPENERS

Brass letter opener with eagle and cornucopia handle, as well as a blade honoring William Taft as president–elect, Ohio Society of New York, December 1908, 10⅛" long, **$75-$100**.

"George Bush-Dan Quayle/ January 20, 1989" inaugural letter opener with wording in 1⅜", plastic-covered, blue disk imbedded in brass frame of opener, 7" long, **$15-$20**.

STAMP HOLDER

Leather stamp holder with celluloid-covered picture of William Taft, circa 1908-'12, 1¾" x 2⅜", **$15-$20**.

NOTEBOOKS

Notebook with James Blaine on cover and John Logan on back, circa 1884, 2¼" x 5¼", **$25-$35**.

Paper notebook with celluloid covers picturing congressional candidate Thomas Scully and a Woodrow Wilson testimonial for Scully, "Whitehead and Hoag Co.," 2" x 3", **$20-$35**.

CALENDARS

"Republican Heritage Calendar" featuring pictures of Richard Nixon-Spiro Agnew, as well as major republican congressional leaders and governors, 1970, 9" x 11⅞", **$10-$20**.

"Quayle-isms" anti-Dan Quayle calendar critically reviewing his quotations, Sterling Calendars, 1992, 11⅞" x 12", circa 1930s, **$10-$20**.

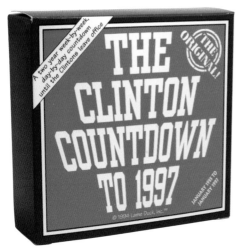

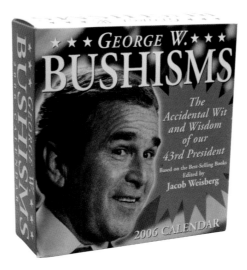

Anti-George W. Bush calendar featuring "The Accidental Wit And Wisdom Of Our 43rd President," in original box, Andrew McMeel Publishing, 5⅜" square, **$10-$20**.

Anti-William Clinton calendar in original box, covering from January 1995 to January 1997, "A Lame Duck Product," circa 1995-'97, 5⅛" x 4⅛", **$10-$20**.

PAPERWEIGHTS

Glass paperweight picturing William McKinley and Garrett Hobart, circa 1896, 4" x 2⅝", **$40-$60**.

Glass paperweight with picture of Theodore Roosevelt, circa 1901-'07, 4" x 2⅝", **$40-$60**.

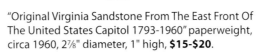

Clear plastic paperweight enclosing "Original White House Material/ Removed In 1950," 3" diameter, 1⅛" high, **$15-$20**.

"Original Virginia Sandstone From The East Front Of The United States Capitol 1793-1960" paperweight, circa 1960, 2⅞" diameter, 1" high, **$15-$20**.

"Ford/ 1976/ Dole" green-tinted-glass paperweight with elephant head image, "Liberty Village," 3⅜" diameter, **$15-$20**.

1992 Republican National Convention, six-sided brass paperweight with stylized elephant wearing cowboy hat, "BFT," 3⅜" x 3", **$10-$20**.

Jimmy Carter for president marble paperweight with enameled red, white and blue brass picture disk attached, 1976, 3⅛" x 2", **$10-$20**.

DESK DISPLAYS AND STATUES

Two Adm. George Dewey metal busts, circa 1899-1900, 1⅞" diameter base, 6" high; and ¼" square base, 3" high, **$20-$30** each.

"Wm. McKinley" copper bust, "H.M.S. & Co.," circa 1896, 2⅞" x 2½" base, 6⅝" high, **$75-$100**.

"Wm. McKinley" metal bust, "G. B. Haines & Co.," circa 1896-1900, 2½" x 2" base, 7" high, **$75-$100**.

Alfred Smith copper-colored plaster bust, circa 1920s, 2½" x 2⅞" base, 4" high, **$20-$30**.

Herbert Hoover brass bust, circa 1928-'32, 1⅝" x 3" base, 5⅝" high, **$75-$100**.

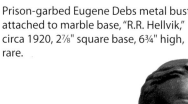

Prison-garbed Eugene Debs metal bust attached to marble base, "R.R. Hellvik," circa 1920, 2⅞" square base, 6¾" high, rare.

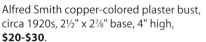

"Franklin D. Roosevelt/ 1933" metal bust, 2" x 1⅝" base, 4½" high, **$35-$50**.

Replica of the Franklin Roosevelt bust erected by the International Ladies Garment Workers at Roosevelt Library, Hyde Park, N.Y., "GD," circa 1940s-'50s, 2⅞" x 2⅞", **$25-$35**.

"F. D. Roosevelt" metal bust, S. M. Colby, circa 1934, 3⅝" x 2 ¾" base, 7¼" high, **$50-$75**; and "Franklin D. Roosevelt" brass bust attached to metal base, Jo Davidson, circa 1934, 3¼" square base, 9¾" high, **$100-$125**.

"The Presidential Star" replica crystal given as gift by President Richard Nixon for 1972 election support, Steuben Glass, circa 1972, 7" high on stand, 6¼" wide, **$35-$50**.

"MacArthur" solid brass bust, circa 1946-'52, 1¼" x 1¼" irregular base, 4" high, **$20-$25**.

TRAVELING VALISE

Simulated-leather valise reading "Volunteer Driver/ 1964 Democratic National Convention/ Atlantic City, N.J.," 15½" x 11", **$10-$25**.

TRASH AND AIR EXPRESS BAGS

"LBJ For The USA" sample trash bag with instructions for ordering more, "Edward Horn Co.," circa 1964, 8⅜" x 10⅝", **$10-$20**.

National Democratic Convention, Air Express net carrying bag, 1964, 14" x 26", **$20-$25**.

WASTEBASKET

Spiro Agnew caricature, multicolored metal wastebasket, "CHEINCO," circa 1968-'72, 10¼" x 6¾" oval, 13" high, **$25-$35**.

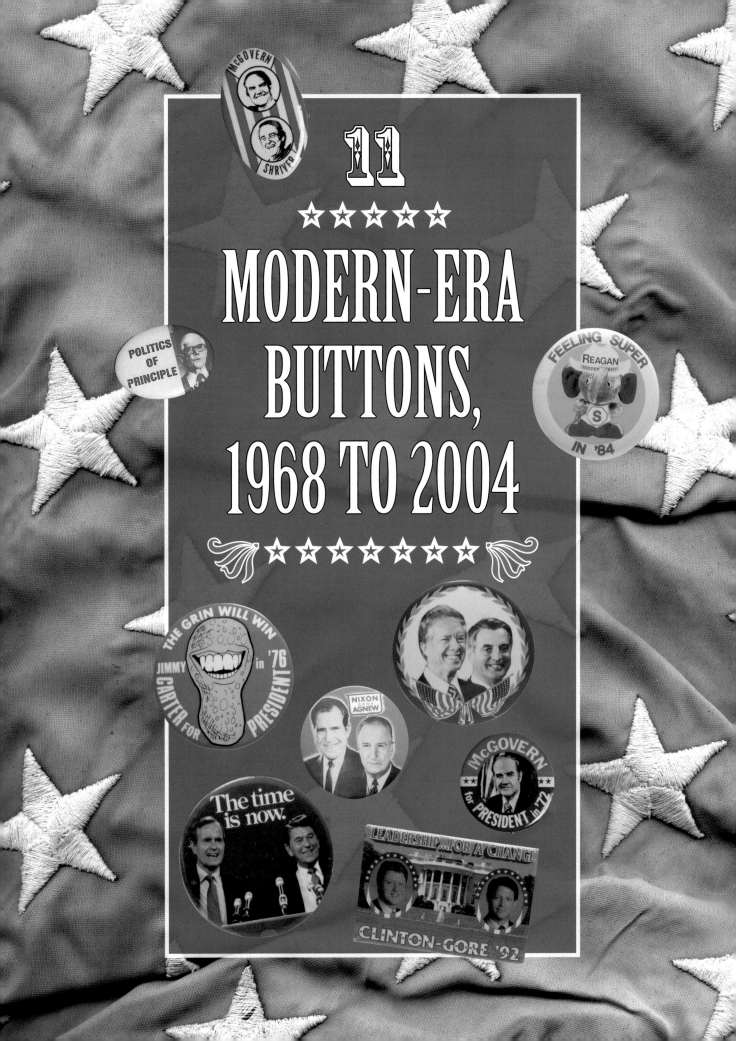

11

☆ ★ ★ ★ ☆

MODERN-ERA BUTTONS, 1968 TO 2004

☆ ★ ★ ★ ★ ★ ★ ☆

For the past four decades, there has been an increase in the number of political campaign buttons designed and produced specifically for the collector market. Commercial entrepreneurs market and sell almost all modern presidential campaign buttons. Rarely do political parties distribute them free of cost, as they had in the past.

As long as buttons are produced before the elections, most collectors accept them as valid items even though the candidates, themselves, had no role in their conception, production or distribution. Button distributors set up kiosks, carts and tables at fairs, political events, flea markets and state and national conventions. Their customers may buy items because they aggressively support the candidates or simply because they want souvenirs.

There is little doubt that some partisans might buy buttons to wear as personal campaign support. More likely, the items go directly into collections.

With the collector in mind, efforts have been made to improve button designs, often by copying the designs of the "Golden Era" of buttons—1896-1916. Sometimes the buttons purposely refer to specific state presidential primaries, debates or other events. The presidential candidate may be pictured with local candidates running for Congress or governor.

The button might also display a well-known musical or motion picture personality. On occasion, a local candidate or member of the campaign staff purposely orders a limited number of coattail buttons with collectors ultimately in mind.

> "Button distributors set up kiosks, carts and tables at fairs, political events, flea markets and conventions."

Richard Nixon, 1968 and 1972.

Hubert Humphrey, 1968.

George Wallace, 1968.

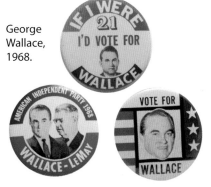

In recent years, some truly beautiful and creative buttons have been offered in extremely limited numbers to increase their desirability and sale potential. A typical, modern, limited-edition button would likely include a statement along its rim that only 200, 100 or even less were produced. Some initially sell for **$5** or more because of their beautiful and clever designs, as well as their rarity.

"Efforts have been made to improve button designs, often by copying those of the "Golden Era" of buttons—1896-1916."

To get a representative sampling of recent buttons, go to the next major American Political Items Collectors (APIC) convention after the election. At the end of the show, usually at least one of the major button distributors has an end-of-the-election quantity sale, with buttons sold at very reasonable prices in order to clear inventory.

As opposed to the "Golden Era" of button manufacture and subsequent collecting, large-sized buttons are not only commonly made and offered today, they are prevalent. When listed for sale, most buttons from the "Modern Era" sell for **$3** to **$6** each, with the earlier pieces usually being on the higher side.

A few particularly rare or unusual ones might sell for much more. This is especially true when a partisan collector determines to have every one of a candidate's buttons. Ultimately you must decide what your preferences are. The following are button samplings from the "Modern Era."

George McGovern, 1972.   Gerald Ford, 1976.

Jimmy Carter, 1976 and 1980.

John Anderson, 1980.

Ronald Reagan, 1980 and 1984.

Walter Mondale, 1984.

Mike Dukakis, 1988.

Ross Perot, 1992.

George H.W. Bush 1988 and 1992.

William Clinton, 1992 and 1996.

Robert Dole, 1996.

Albert Gore, 2000.

George W. Bush, 2000 and 2004.

John Kerry, 2004.

12

FAKES, FANTASIES

and

REPRODUCTIONS

BY MARK CHERVENKA

Many previous books on political collectibles mention how to detect new buttons, but few discuss fakes made in glass, china and other materials. Non-button political collectibles, generally referred to as three-dimensional or 3-D, are some of the more difficult pieces for collectors to authenticate. If a collector questions a button, there are many excellent button reference books with which to compare suspected fakes to originals. Authenticating 3-D is much more difficult. Most 3-D fakes are often "fantasy" items—those with no original counterparts for comparison.

The 3-D political fakes shown here are but a sample of what's been circulating in the market. Some have been sold as old through honest mistakes, and others are consistently misrepresented as old by unethical sellers.

New campaign flags are printed on one side only. The colors from the front do not go through to the back. Note the jagged "pinked" edge on the new flag.

Other new flags include: a portrait of U.S. Grant, "1861-1865, Let Us Have Peace;" Lincoln, portrait surrounded by white stars, "Lincoln & Hamlin;" William H. Harrison, portrait, "The Hero of Tippecanoe;" James K. Polk, portrait surrounded by white stars, "Polk and Dallas;" bearded Abraham Lincoln portrait in oval medallion, 33 white stars in union; Henry Clay, portrait, surrounded by white stars in union, "Clay and Frelinghuysen;" and "Lincoln and Hamlin," 30 white stars in union.

The new cotton flag, 6" x 9", is copied from an original used in the campaign of 1860.

Pictured here is the original counterpart, 36" x 26", to the new flag in the photo at left. Size alone is not an indication of age.

FLAGS

There are a variety of new political campaign flags being made. Originals of these flags can run from hundreds of dollars to tens of thousands of dollars. A New York State firm makes at least 18 new flags that sell for as little as $10 each.

Original campaign banners resembling American flags were used primarily from about 1840 to the beginning of the 20th century. The typical form was to overprint the flag with the candidates' portraits and campaign slogans. Most vintage campaign flags were made of cotton, but some were made of silk or other fabrics.

The majority of authentic flags were commercially manufactured, although some were homemade, especially before 1840. Slogans and portraits on virtually all the commercially made flags were created by printing, not weaving. That is to say slogans and portraits were printed with inks on the surface of the fabric, not created by weaving threads within the fabric.

Although most new flags are relatively small, about 9 inches wide each, size alone is not a reliable test of age. Vintage political campaign flags appear in a wide variety of sizes from as small as 8 x 5 inches to large enough to cover the side of a horse-drawn wagon.

Disregarding size, there are several reliable tests that can quickly help separate reproductions from the originals. First, insist any framing around the flag be removed. You cannot see the edges and back of a flag when it is framed. Edges and the reverse side must be visible for an accurate examination.

Edges of the great majority of new flags, for example, are "pinked," not hemmed. Pinking is a textile term referring to a jagged-edged cut that helps prevent unraveling. Edges of authentic commercially manufactured campaign flags are almost always finished with the fabric folded over and hemmed, not pinked. Most new flags, especially in online auctions, are framed and matted so the jagged pinked edge is not always apparent.

Most new flags are commercially manufactured by printing inks on sheets of cotton. The cotton is rather coarse, averaging only about 70 threads per square inch. It is an unglazed dull finish. The blue canton and red stripes appear only on the front side of the new flags. Inks or dyes used

> "Edges of the great majority of new flags are 'pinked,' not hemmed."

John C. Breckinridge, 1860 presidential candidate of the Southern Democratic Party, is one of the images now appearing in fake Stanhope lenses inserted into genuinely old objects like this Civil War-era minié ball.

in the cantons and red stripes of vintage flags are visible on both sides, not just the front. Portraits and slogans, though, appear on only the front sides of both old and new flags.

STANHOPE LENSES

A picture of John C. Breckinridge, 1860 presidential candidate of the Southern Democratic Party and a Confederate Civil War general, is one of the images now appearing in new Stanhope lenses.

Stanhopes, miniature images viewed through a magnifying lens, were first produced in the mid 1800s. Reproduction Stanhope lenses with images of famous political and historical figures have been available since the late 1990s. Besides Breckinridge, other new images include those of Abraham Lincoln, Jefferson Davis, Nathan Bedford Forrest, Abner Doubleday, Robert E. Lee and many others.

New images can be purchased already mounted in stock items or they can be inserted into customer-supplied objects. The Breckinridge example shown here is mounted in a genuine 1860s era *minié ball*—a 19th-century conical rifle bullet with a hollow base that expanded when fired.

Other new images of political and historical figures have been found inset into Civil War-style buckles and knife handles. New images set in minié balls have sold for $200 to over $400 on eBay, the online auction site. Other new Stanhopes with political images have appeared in fixed-price catalogs, or at political shows and other venues.

In original 19th century Stanhopes, the image was formed on a photographic emulsion that coated a tiny block of glass. A miniature lens was then glued over the image to provide magnification. Images in modern reproductions are on a separate tiny piece of film, not emulsion, which is mounted under a miniature lens. There is no practical way to separate new from old once the image is mounted in objects.

While there are authentic 19th- and early-20th-century vintage Stanhopes mounted in minié balls, subjects in the vintage pieces are quite different from the new Stanhopes. The vast majority of authentic Stanhopes found in minié balls are scenic views of battlefields, not portraits of individual political or military figures. The battlefields depicted in authentic Stanhopes are almost always either Gettysburg or Antietam.

Several of these authentic battlefield images do include pictures of generals, but only as part of the battlefield scenes, not as individual portraits. As a general rule, any Stanhope with a single image of a political figure or Civil War general should be considered suspect unless the seller can prove otherwise. This is particularly true of more obscure figures like Abner Doubleday, George Thomas, John Breckinridge and other figures virtually unknown to the general public.

Images of such figures have significance only for collectors and are apparently targeted to appeal to that market. Original Stanhopes were inexpensive souvenirs designed to appeal to a mass market, not collectors.

Edges in genuine tintypes, top, were hidden under plate holders and left unexposed. They form dark borders (arrows) on original tintypes. Images in most new fakes like this faked Grant cover the entire surface with no sign of the dark borders left by original plate holders. Scratches in the surfaces of most new images also reveal a white background. Backgrounds behind scratches in nearly all originals are dark brown or black, not white.

A fake 4 ¼-inch pottery elephant marked "GOP" in raised, molded letters on the side, its base is marked "McCoy," yet it is not an original McCoy piece.

This 6-inch, frosted-glass figure of Abraham Lincoln was made by the L.E. Smith Glass Co. in the 1970s. It was part of a four-piece set commemorating the presidents on Mt. Rushmore, with the others, of course, including Thomas Jefferson, George Washington and Theodore Roosevelt. It is often confused with 19ᵗʰ-century Gillinder Glass Co. solid, frosted-glass busts with rectangular bases.

TINTYPES

There are a number of quite good fakes of politically related tintypes on the market. The best are those made from genuinely old tintypes from which the original emulsion and image have been removed. After cleaning, a new photographic emulsion is added to the old plate. The plate is then treated like photographic paper and exposed under a darkroom enlarger holding a film negative. Finally, the plate is developed just like paper.

Film negatives can be obtained by using either a regular 35mm film camera or digital camera. Typical sources of images are auction catalogs, reference books or genuine originals. Once photographed, the image may or may not be altered with digital imaging software to add or erase backgrounds, apply medals or flags, make repairs or other work to increase the value. Film negatives are ready for immediate use, and digital files are converted to film negatives.

Many of the better fakes can be detected by looking at the edges of the tintypes. At least one edge and usually more than one edge of an original tintype is almost always hidden by the plate holder and never exposed. The unexposed areas show up as dark bands or stripes on the final images, like those in the original tintype at the top of the previous page.

In most fakes, as with the Grant tintype at the bottom of the previous page, the image extends across the entire surface and does not show any signs of having been in a plate holder.

Removing some emulsion on the fake Grant tintype reveals a white surface behind the image. The metal sheets used for authentic tintypes were painted black or dark brown, or Japanned, before being covered with photographic emulsion.

Scratches in the emulsion of original images should produce dark lines and spots, not a white background. Clipped corners are normal in genuine tintypes. Tintypes were trimmed to fit cases and mats, so trimming is not a factor in determining age.

Images obtained from publications printed on printing presses, like reference books and auction catalogs, are also good indicators of fakes. Printed images are broken into tiny dots of black, or screened, to create the illusion of a continuous tone photograph. The dots are often captured in the film negative and transferred to the image in the final tintype. If the image on the tintype is composed of tiny dots, a screened image, it is a fake. Look at black and white newspaper photos for examples of screened images.

GLASS AND POTTERY

The frosted-glass statue of Abraham Lincoln in the accompanying photo is frequently represented as a 19ᵗʰ-century product of Gillinder Glass Co. of Philadelphia. The statue of Abraham Lincoln and three similar busts of Thomas Jefferson, George Washington and Theodore Roosevelt are not Gillinder. The four-piece set was made by L.E. Smith Glass in the mid-1970s to commemorate Mt. Rushmore.

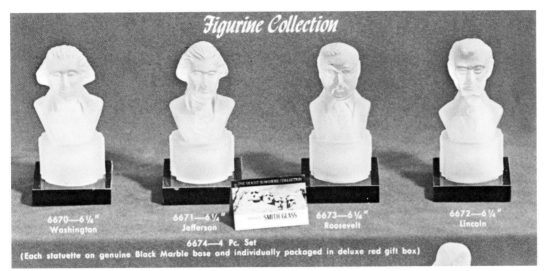

These are the frosted-glass Mt. Rushmore presidents, as shown in a 1974 L.E. Smith Glass Co. catalog.

The L.E. Smith Glass pieces were introduced shortly before the Bicentennial when there was quite a bit of interest in American history and patriotic symbols. Gillinder, officially Gillinder & Sons, of Philadelphia, did make frosted glass busts of three American presidents—Lincoln, Ulysses Grant and Washington—but never in the shapes of the Smith figures. All the Smith figures are hollow with cylindrical bases. Authentic Gillinder busts of presidents are solid glass with rectangular bases.

Unlike the frosted-glass bust of Lincoln, which is a legitimate 30-plus-year-old glass collectible, another widely seen piece of political glass is a notorious fake. It is a bottle made of white glass sold as a Calvin Coolidge campaign item. This is a fantasy item; no vintage counterpart exists. The Coolidge bottles have been on the market since the 1970s.

Another widespread fantasy political item is a pottery elephant bank marked "GOP" on the side and "McCoy" on the base. The fantasy elephant bank causes problems for collectors of political items, as well as McCoy pottery enthusiasts.

The original McCoy Pottery factory, which closed in the 1960s, never made such an item. The fakes are produced in a small pottery facility in Ohio, which is using the McCoy mark on many pieces. The only similar, vintage product is a small 2-inch pottery elephant standing on four legs made by Morton Pottery, not McCoy.

Morton manufactured elephants from the late 1930s through the 1950s, with each elephant having "GOP" molded on its side and almost always a candidate's name on the other side. Most candidates were involved in local and state races, yet some Morton elephants featured candidates for U.S. Senate, including Everett Dirkson.

A fantasy bottle purportedly from the Calvin Coolidge campaign of 1924, the 6-inch-high, opaque, white glass piece has no vintage counterpart, and has been on the market since at least the mid 1970s.

BUTTONS

Buttons are the most reproduced of all political campaign collectibles. Even experienced buyers can be fooled by sophisticated and deliberate fakes. But an average collector or beginner just getting starting isn't likely to see many

> "Buttons are the most reproduced of all political campaign collectibles."

elaborately made forgeries. He or she is much more likely to have problems with mass-produced, modern reproductions, such as the campaign buttons found at flea markets, garage sales and in online auctions.

The majority of reproduced political buttons were never originally sold or represented as old. Many of the confusing new buttons on the market were originally used in advertising and sales promotions during presidential election years.

Some of the companies that have issued more modern political advertising buttons include United States Boraxo Co.; American Oil Co. (AMOCO); Art Fair; Liberty Mint; Westinghouse; Kimberly Clark (Kleenex); Crackerbarrel; Proctor & Gamble; and Seagram, besides many more. Most buttons issued by these companies were distributed in the 1960s and early 1970s. Now that they have been around for over 30 years, many show up in online auctions described as "antiques."

Offered by AMOCO in 1972, this is a reproduction of a political button with its original advertising header.

The reproduction AMOCO pin, bottom of previous page, is at first glance quite similar to the vintage Alton Parker, here. The colored printing on the William McKinley-Theodore Roosevelt pin shows the tiny dot pattern of modern process color printing. The colored areas on the Parker pin are solid blocks of ink without dots.

Here's a general checklist that will help you detect most of the new buttons previously described.

1. Any button with the name of any of the businesses listed on the previous page is modern. An Honest Abe button marked AMOCO is obviously new. Similarly, any button that includes the image or name of a modern product such as Kleenex is new.

2. Any button marked "Reproduction" is new, although this word is sometimes deliberately erased or painted over.

3. Compare the size of the suspected button to a known original in a political reference book. Many sets of new buttons were made all the same size regardless of the size of the original button.

4. Know what material was used to make the original button. Celluloid buttons weren't widely available until about 1896. The 1960s celluloid buttons by Art Fair, for example, depicting candidates who ran before that date, are obviously new. Conversely, many new buttons lithographed on metal were originally made of celluloid. Again, materials and lists of candidates are easily found in books on political collectibles.

5. Vintage buttons have signs of normal wear consistent with their age. Original metal buttons often have slight rust in the back. Metal rings around original celluloid buttons should show slight oxidation and tarnishing. Genuine rust and wear is scatted and random. Metal surfaces that are entirely worn or completely rusted have usually been intentionally altered by mechanical or chemical means.

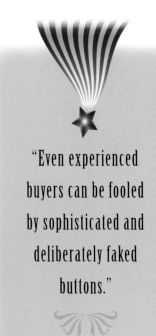

"Even experienced buyers can be fooled by sophisticated and deliberately faked buttons."

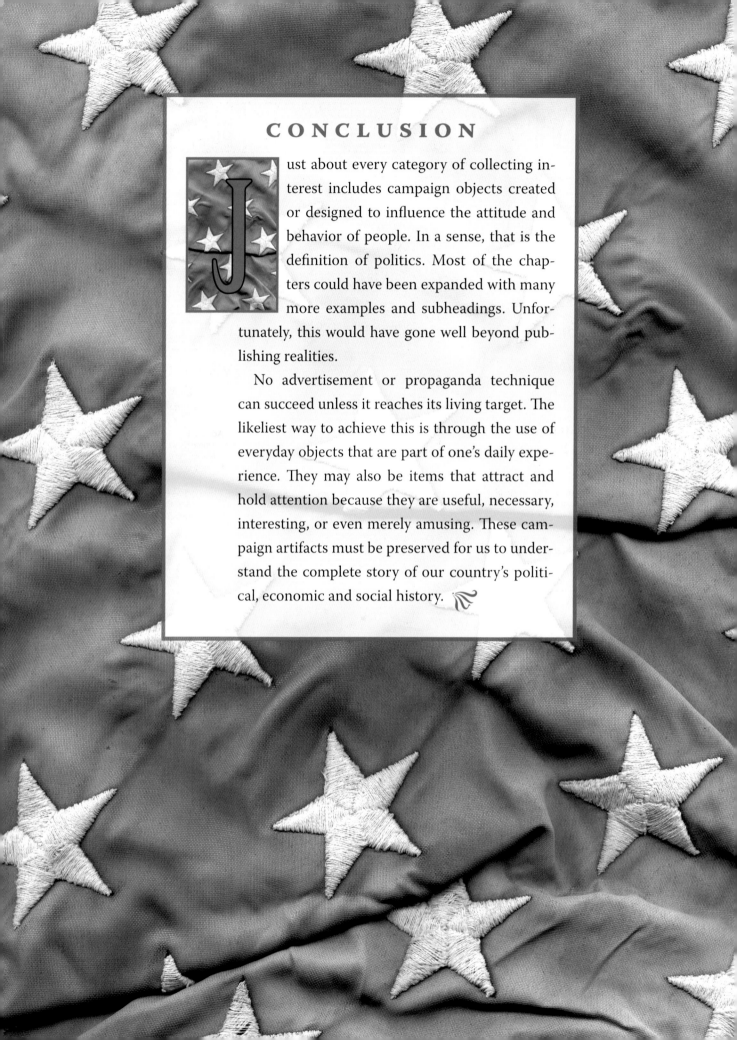

CONCLUSION

Just about every category of collecting interest includes campaign objects created or designed to influence the attitude and behavior of people. In a sense, that is the definition of politics. Most of the chapters could have been expanded with many more examples and subheadings. Unfortunately, this would have gone well beyond publishing realities.

No advertisement or propaganda technique can succeed unless it reaches its living target. The likeliest way to achieve this is through the use of everyday objects that are part of one's daily experience. They may also be items that attract and hold attention because they are useful, necessary, interesting, or even merely amusing. These campaign artifacts must be preserved for us to understand the complete story of our country's political, economic and social history.

MORE RELIABLE REFERENCES FOR YOUR HOBBY INTERESTS

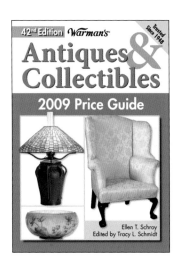

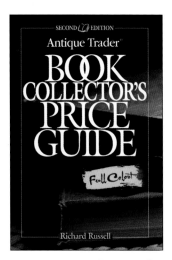

Warman's® Antiques & Collectibles 2009 Price Guide

42nd Edition

by Ellen T. Schroy and Tracy L. Schmidt

As the longest-running antique price guide, this newest edition features 2,400 color photos, an easy-to-use format and tens of thousands of listings. Bonus information is included on fakes and reproductions.

Softcover • 7 x 10 • 800 pages
2,400 color photos
Item# Z1696 • $24.99

Antique Trader® Book Collector's Price Guide

2nd Edition

by Richard Russell

This full-color edition covers a variety of books, from Americana to science fiction, including 6,000+ updated values, rarities listings, and pseudonym guide.

Softcover • 6 x 9 • 448 pages
1,000 color photos
Item# ATBK2 • $24.99

Warman's® Field Guide to Precious Moments®

Values and Identification

by Mary Sieber

Accurately assess the value of your Precious Moments figurines, ornaments, plates and more, with the 2,000+ listings, secondary market values and 250 color photos in this portable book.

Softcover • 4-3/16 x 5-3/16 • 512 pages
250 color photos
Item# Z1778 • $12.99

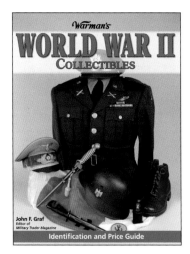

Warman's® World War II Collectibles

Identification and Price Guide

by John F. Graf

Get pricing and historical details about World War II collectibles such as helmets, uniforms, firearms, daggers and mementos, in this extensive full-color book.

Softcover • 8-1/4 x 10-7/8 • 256 pages
1,000 color photos
Item# Z0972 • $24.99

Collector's Guide to PEZ

Values & Identification
3rd Edition

by Shawn Peterson

Explore PEZ company history while identifying and assessing the PEZ containers in your possession, using the 1,000 fun color photos and listings of common and exquisitely rare PEZ.

Softcover • 8-1/4 x 10-7/8 • 256 pages
1,000 color photos
Item# Z1843 • $24.99